National
4 & 5

Administration and IT

Anne Bradley
Adam Stephenson

Photo credits

Chapter opening images: p.1 and p.14 © Joss – Fotolia.com; p.26, p.55 and p.71 © Tinka – Fotolia.com; p.89, p.93 and p.108 © Scanrail – Fotolia.com. p.8 (from top) © terex – iStockphoto, © trekandshoot – Fotolia.com, © Hodder Gibson, © Radharc Images / Alamy; p.10 (left) © KURTAY / Alamy, (right top) © Viper – Fotolia.com, (right bottom) © Hodder Gibson; p.11 (from top) © Iakov Filimonov – Fotolia.com, © Universal Images Group Limited / Alamy, © Artur Golbert – Thinkstock, © Tom Perkins / Fotolia.com; p.55 (right) © AlphaAndOmega / Alamy, (left) © Leslie Garland Picture Library / Alamy; p.109 (both) Screenshot taken by Sharon McTeir; p.110 (both) Screenshot taken by Sharon McTeir; p.111 (both) Screenshot taken by Sharon McTeir; p.112 (all) Screenshot taken by Sharon McTeir.

Screenshots from Microsoft products are used with permission from Microsoft.

Every effort has been made to trace all copyright holders, but if any have been inadvertently overlooked the Publishers will be pleased to make the necessary arrangements at the first opportunity.

Although every effort has been made to ensure that website addresses are correct at time of going to press, Hodder Gibson cannot be held responsible for the content of any website mentioned in this book. It is sometimes possible to find a relocated web page by typing in the address of the home page for a website in the URL window of your browser.

Hachette UK's policy is to use papers that are natural, renewable and recyclable products and made from wood grown in sustainable forests. The logging and manufacturing processes are expected to conform to the environmental regulations of the country of origin.

Orders: please contact Bookpoint Ltd, 130 Park Drive, Abingdon, Oxon OX14 4SE. Telephone: (44) 01235 827720. Fax: (44) 01235 400454. Lines are open 9.00–5.00, Monday to Saturday, with a 24-hour message answering service. Visit our website at www.hoddereducation.co.uk. Hodder Gibson can be contacted direct on: Tel: 0141 848 1609; Fax: 0141 889 6315; email: hoddergibson@hodder.co.uk

© Anne Bradley and Adam Stephenson 2014

First published in 2014 by

Hodder Gibson, an imprint of Hodder Education,

An Hachette UK Company

2a Christie Street

Paisley PA1 1NB

Impression number 5 4 3 2 1

Year 2018 2017 2016 2015 2014

All rights reserved. Apart from any use permitted under UK copyright law, no part of this publication may be reproduced or transmitted in any form or by any means, electronic or mechanical, including photocopying and recording, or held within any information storage and retrieval system, without permission in writing from the publisher or under licence from the Copyright Licensing Agency Limited. Further details of such licences (for reprographic reproduction) may be obtained from the Copyright Licensing Agency Limited, Saffron House, 6–10 Kirby Street, London EC1N 8TS.

Cover photo © Getty Images / iStockphoto / Thinkstock

Illustrations by Barking Dog Art and Integra Software Services Pvt. Ltd.

Typeset in 11/12.65 pt Stempel Schneidler Std Light by Integra Software Services Pvt. Ltd., Pondicherry, India

Printed in Italy

A catalogue record for this title is available from the British Library

ISBN: 978 1444 184266

Contents

Teacher's introduction

This book is intended for use in the classroom by students and teachers alike. It has been written primarily to support the Scottish Qualifications Authority (SQA) National 4 and National 5 level Administration and IT courses, as outlined for first implementation in 2014. It should be noted, however, that the Chapters referring to specific IT skills could be used for students on Level 3 and Level 4 Business and/or IT courses.

The book has been written in simple everyday language and every effort has been made to include essential terminology. We have attempted to include information that is as relevant and recent as possible prior to publication as well as references to websites which are up-to-date at publication. The book is suitable for use as a classroom resource or as a text for students to work through by themselves. Every effort has been made to include all elements of knowledge and skills required for the study of Administration and IT. Electronic files for some of the tasks are available to download, free of charge, from **www.hoddergibson.co.uk/updatesandextras**, but it should be noted that, in line with the aims and objectives of the course, specific solutions are not provided.

Each chapter in this book has been structured in the same way and comprises:

- learning intentions
- specific knowledge and understanding content
- information points to reinforce learning
- terminology specific to the course
- simple Tasks designed to *practically* assess learning at both National 4 and National 5.

In addition, the Chapters concerning IT skills contain step by step guides to help develop essential skills required by the course – to ensure that all students can complete IT tasks to a professional standard.

It is hoped that the National 4 and National 5 Practice Tasks included at the end of the book will provide both student and teacher with enough practice to be able to prepare for the challenge of the National 4 Added Value Unit/National 5 Assignment.

Finally, a glossary of essential terminology is provided.

We hope that you will find this book a useful resource in the delivery of National 4 and National 5 Administration and IT courses.

Anne Bradley

Adam Stephenson

February 2014

Unit 1

Administrative Practices

Chapter 1

Administration in the workplace

By the end of this chapter you will be able to demonstrate an understanding of:

- ✓ the tasks, skills and qualities of an administrative assistant
- ✓ the features of good customer care
- ✓ the responsibilities of employers and employees in terms of health and safety in the workplace
- ✓ the responsibilities of employers and employees in terms of security of people in the workplace
- ✓ the responsibilities of employers and employees in terms of security of property in the workplace
- ✓ the responsibilities of employers and employees in terms of security of information in the workplace.

An **Administrative Assistant** (usually referred to as an Admin Assistant) provides support to specific departments or teams within an organisation.

In order to be a successful Admin Assistant, certain skills and qualities are required. When organisations are looking for an Admin Assistant, it is important that the basic tasks, skills and qualities required are identified – this is usually done in the form of a **job analysis**.

Once this is done a **job description** would be prepared, containing basic information about the job, for example job title, rate of pay and a description of the main tasks of the job.

Sometimes it is important that the right type of person is chosen and to assist in this a **person specification** would also be prepared. This would contain information on the type of person required, including qualifications, skills and qualities. Sometimes special skills or experience will be mentioned, for example a good working knowledge of **spreadsheets** and **databases**.

A *skill* is something that you can learn and become better at with practice. A *quality*, on the other hand, refers to a personal characteristic that you have.

Using the information gathered in these two documents, a **job advert** would then be created and uploaded to a jobs website or sent to a local newspaper.

National 4 & 5 task

Search the internet to find a job advert for an Admin Assistant in your local area. Print out the chosen web page.

Skills Checklist

Be good at:

- ✓ dealing with people in the workplace
- ✓ planning work to meet deadlines
- ✓ using the computer to make new documents
- ✓ using the computer to make changes to documents
- ✓ processing business documents according to company procedure
- ✓ organising and storing files in a proper order.

Qualities Checklist

- ✓ Good social skills:
  - patient
  - friendly
  - tactful
  - discreet
  - approachable
  - able to work alone or as part of a team.
- ✓ Attention to detail.
- ✓ Focus on tasks being done.

The role of the Admin Assistant is very varied and depends upon the type of office you work in. Some offices deal with confidential work and therefore discretion is more important, whereas other offices deal with more routine tasks.

Tasks	Skills/Qualities	Why?
Requesting assistance from a member of staff to make up packs for a meeting.	Approachable, organised, able to work as part of a team.	Good relationships with other staff is important to make sure the office is run smoothly.
Creating a to-do list.	Organised, good time management.	Good planning is important to allow the efficient completion of work.
Entering details of a meeting into an e-diary.	IT skills – *See Chapter 8.*	
Filing information manually.	Organised.	Regular filing should become part of the everyday routine to ensure important documents are not lost.
Updating a database with details of a member of staff's new address.	Be discreet. IT skills – *See Chapter 4.*	When dealing with personal information it is important that the Admin Assistant does not pass on any information.
Using word processing to prepare business documents.	Good literacy skills. IT skills – *See Chapter 5.*	Good planning is important to allow the office to run smoothly.
Receiving and making telephone calls.	Social skills – pleasant, polite, good communicator.	Give a good impression of the company to customers and callers.
Checking expenses claimed against the company's policy.	Attention to detail, accuracy – details of spending and calculations of amounts being claimed.	Companies will have rules about what staff can and cannot claim for and the Admin Assistant will have to make sure these rules are followed.
Booking accommodation/travel according to the company's policy.	Attention to detail, following specific instructions.	
Using a spreadsheet to assist with budgeting and other calculations.	Good numeracy skills. IT skills – *See Chapter 3.*	Business documents need to be accurate to be useful.

Examples of tasks linking skills and qualities

National 4 task

Let's check to see if you know what the ideal Admin Assistant would be like. Complete the following task using the file **Ideal Person**.

Ideal Person

The ideal person for the job of Administrative Assistant should have the following:

Skills and Qualities

complete four possible suggestions below

1.
2.
3.
4.

and

should also have some qualifications such as:

Qualifications

complete four possible qualifications below

1.
2.
3.
4.

National 5 task

Prepare an A4 booklet-style induction leaflet outlining the duties of the Admin Assistant job that could be given to new Admin Assistants. Make sure you make full use of the space and also use a variety of fonts and graphics. Your name should appear in the footer of each page. Use the following information to complete the leaflet.

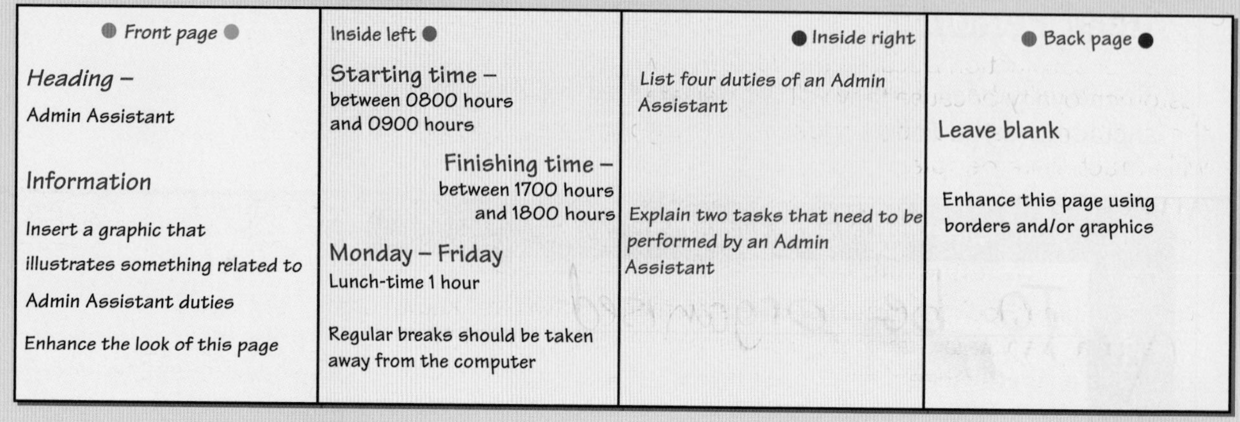

Front page	Inside left	Inside right	Back page
Heading – Admin Assistant Information Insert a graphic that illustrates something related to Admin Assistant duties Enhance the look of this page	Starting time – between 0800 hours and 0900 hours Finishing time – between 1700 hours and 1800 hours Monday – Friday Lunch-time 1 hour Regular breaks should be taken away from the computer	List four duties of an Admin Assistant Explain two tasks that need to be performed by an Admin Assistant	Leave blank Enhance this page using borders and/or graphics

Customer care

Customer care is a way of working which helps to enhance the level of customer satisfaction – *that is, the feeling that a product or service has met the customer's expectation.*

> Each and every communication with a customer is a chance to impress or to disappoint.

An Admin Assistant communicates with lots of people, therefore good communication skills need to be developed. Within the organisation, communication has to take place, but this is often informal, for example a chat with a colleague or a short email. When dealing with customers or callers, however, a more professional approach is required. So that this can be achieved, most organisations create a list of guidelines for any member of staff who has contact with customers outside the company – usually called **company policy**.

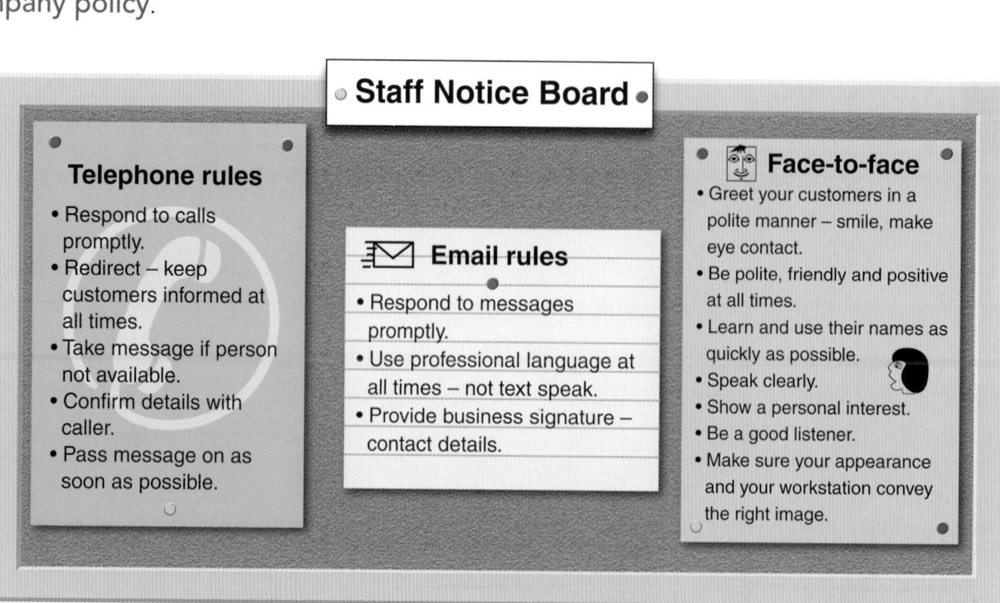

Staff Notice Board
Telephone rules
• Respond to calls promptly.
• Redirect – keep customers informed at all times.
• Take message if person not available.
• Confirm details with caller.
• Pass message on as soon as possible.
Email rules
• Respond to messages promptly.
• Use professional language at all times – not text speak.
• Provide business signature – contact details.
Face-to-face
• Greet your customers in a polite manner – smile, make eye contact.
• Be polite, friendly and positive at all times.
• Learn and use their names as quickly as possible.
• Speak clearly.
• Show a personal interest.
• Be a good listener.
• Make sure your appearance and your workstation convey the right image.

Benefits of good customer service

Research into effective customer service shows that:

- keeping a current customer is much easier and cheaper than attracting a new one
- a company can build up a good reputation for providing excellent service.

> Keeping your promises is most important of all. Promise only what you know you can achieve.

Providing excellent customer service will increase:

- customer satisfaction *because* the customer will be happy to use the company
- customer loyalty *because* they will be prepared to come back again and again
- the number of new customers *because* the good reputation of the company will attract more people.

National 4 & 5 task

Using the internet, look for customer care statements of two well-known organisations. Using this information as inspiration, compose a similar statement that you think would be suitable for your school. Present this on an A4 sheet (landscape format) – this should be easy to read if posted on a noticeboard.

Impact of poor customer service

Organisations cannot survive without customers. If the customer is not happy, he or she will take their business elsewhere! The lack of returning customers and poor reputation will result in poor profits and possible closure.

Customer care Q&A session

Q – What is a customer care policy?
A – A customer care policy is a set of guidelines to help support and deal with clients or customers in any business or organisation.
Q – Why is it important to have a customer care policy?
A – A good customer care policy will keep clients coming back and a bad one will keep them away.
Q – What does customer care actually involve?
A – Customer care usually involves helping out the customers by answering any questions they may have; providing support if they need it; and assisting them if they have any problems with the business and its products or services.
Q – What is another name for customer care?
A – Customer service: sometimes organisations have a customer service policy.
Q – What is the most important skill required to give good customer care?
A – Good communication skills are essential to deliver good customer care – the ability to listen, understand and talk to the customer.
Q – Anything else?
A – It is important to have a very good knowledge of the product/service, so that any questions can be answered quickly and efficiently.
Q – Are there any other qualities that are useful?
A – Patience – probably the most important of all, especially if the customer is irritated or annoyed about the situation. A calm and polite manner can help to smooth over a difficult situation.

Read the case study below and complete the tasks which follow.

The ABC software company designs and develops software products. It is a very modern company and employs over a hundred people.

Recently, the company released a new exciting software product. The product was very popular, with a high demand at the beginning.

However, after a few months, customers started calling the company with some questions about the product. There was no answer. Most people thought it was because the company was very busy. The customers tried again, but still no reply. The customers sent emails, texts and letters; but they were ignored.

This made the customers unhappy and they stopped buying that product. Though the product was very useful, people stopped buying it because there was no after-sales support. The company had neglected one main aspect — customer care!

This proved costly for the company and it had to shut down. Obviously, any company wins or loses depending on its customer care.

National 4 task

Design a poster to be displayed on the staff noticeboard to help staff with delivering good customer care. Use the file **Customer Care** to help with the contents of the poster and include the customer care statement from the previous task.

Hints for delivering good customer care	Complete four possible suggestions below.

National 5 task

Prepare an A4 booklet-style customer care leaflet which is to be used at the next staff training day event – Customer Service Training. Make sure you make full use of the space and also use a variety of fonts and graphics. Your name should appear in the footer of each page. Use the information at the top of the opposite page to complete the leaflet.

● Front page ●	Inside left ●	● Inside right	● Back page ●
Heading – Customer Service Training *[insert the date – first Monday of next month]* *Insert a graphic that illustrates good customer care* *Enhance the look of this page*	List four suggestions for the delivery of good customer care Use a suitable font/colour to show the importance of these points	*Outline the benefits of good customer care* *Describe the consequences of poor customer care to the organisation*	Insert the mission statement previously created Enhance this page using borders and/or graphics

Health and safety

Most organisations have a written policy on health and safety issues, which is made available to all staff. It is important that all staff comply with the policy.

It is important that everyone (employers and employees) is aware of their responsibilities in terms of:

- health and safety
- security of people
- security of property
- security of information.

Health and safety in the workplace is the responsibility of *everyone* in the workplace.

To work safely, it is important that employees are aware of their responsibilities not only to themselves but also to others around them.

Did you know that in 2009/2010:

- 1.2 million working people were suffering from a work-related illness
- 175 workers were killed at work
- 115,000 workplace injuries were reported
- 26.4 million working days were lost due to work-related illness and workplace injury
- workplace injuries and ill health cost society an estimated £14 billion?

Visit **www.hse.gov.uk/aboutus/realpeople/** for more information about health and safety.

It is also important that organisations make sure that they provide a safe workplace for all. The Health and Safety Executive (HSE) is the government organisation involved in the promotion of health and safety. Its responsibilities span every type of business – from the most hazardous industry to low-risk environments such as offices.

Hazards in the workplace

A hazard is something which causes injury or harm to an employee while working.

Workstation		
Potential hazard Unsuitable chairs, size and placement of desks, overloaded sockets, unsuitable location of sockets, bad lighting, trailing cables, personal items on floor.	**Solution** Check position and layout of workstation, identify hazards and report them to management.	
Storage		
	**Potential hazard** Papers lying about, overloaded cabinets, items stored out of reach.	**Solution** Keep work area tidy, do not overfill bins, don't stack paper too high, use kick stool to access items stored out of reach.
Equipment		
Potential hazard Faulty equipment. No appropriate safety attachments.	**Solution** Put a sign on faulty equipment and report to employer. Ask employer to provide suitable adjustable equipment, such as anti-glare screen, wrist rests.	
Working practices		
	**Potential hazard** Obstructed fire doors, corridors, fire exits.	**Solution** Refer to H&S Guidelines which will state that fire doors should be kept clear at all times and must not be propped open at any time. Notices to remind staff of this should be displayed clearly.

H&S guidelines

The current legislation for health and safety at work outlines the following provisions.

Responsibilities of employee (worker)	Responsibilities of employer (organisation)
• Co-operate with the organisation on health and safety matters • Take reasonable care of his or her health and safety • Take reasonable care of other workers' health and safety • Must NOT interfere with or misuse anything provided for health and safety purposes	• Provide safe entrance and exit from workplace • Provide safe working conditions/methods of working • Provide safe, properly maintained equipment • Arrange the safe use, storage and movement of hazardous substances • Provide protective clothing where necessary • Provide training and information on health and safety • Provide up-to-date health and safety policy – to all staff • Appoint a properly qualified safety representative

National 4 & 5 task

The Health and Safety Executive (HSE) website provides leaflets that give specific information for all types of workers. Admin Assistants work with computers (doing IT tasks) for a lot of their working day. Visit **www.hse.gov.uk** and search 'working with VDUs'. Download and save the free leaflet, which gives lots of information on health and safety issues when using a computer at work.

Save with the filename **HSE Working with VDUs**.

National 4 task

Search the HSE website to find the leaflet with information about the rights and responsibilities of workers – *Your health, your safety: A brief guide for workers*. Prepare a presentation – using suitable software – to be used at an induction day for new staff. Include a maximum of five slides, and include a link to the HSE web page you are using for your presentation.

National 5 task

Search the HSE website to find the leaflet with information about the rights and responsibilities of employers – *Health and Safety made Simple*. Prepare a presentation – using suitable software – to be used at a training day for managers. Include a maximum of five slides, and include a link to the HSE web page you are using for your presentation.

Security of people, property and information

Security of people, property and information is the responsibility of *everyone* in the workplace.

People

Organisations will provide procedures or rules that employees must follow to make sure that everyone in the workplace is safe and secure. It is important to make sure that only authorised people can get into a building, not only when the business is closed but also during the working day.

The basic requirements of employees are as follows:

- Sign in when entering the building and of course sign out when leaving.
- Wear ID badges at all times – this allows people to recognise fellow workers.
- Report and/or challenge people who are not wearing ID badges.
- Escort visitors around the workplace.

And the organisation can help by providing the following:

- Controlled entry – using an intercom system to allow entry.
- Security doors with pin codes or swipe passes at the entrance and around the building to prevent strangers entering the building or moving through it.

It is the responsibility of the organisation to produce a procedure for staff to follow to ensure their safety. They must also provide staff with badges and a security system to restrict unauthorised access.

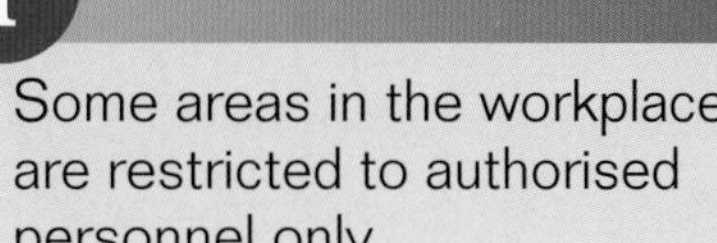

Some areas in the workplace are restricted to authorised personnel only.

Dealing with visitors

Visitors to a business must be treated in a welcoming and professional manner. They can be customers, suppliers or people coming to be interviewed. Whatever the reason, the organisation must ensure that they are genuine visitors. There are some simple rules that can be applied:

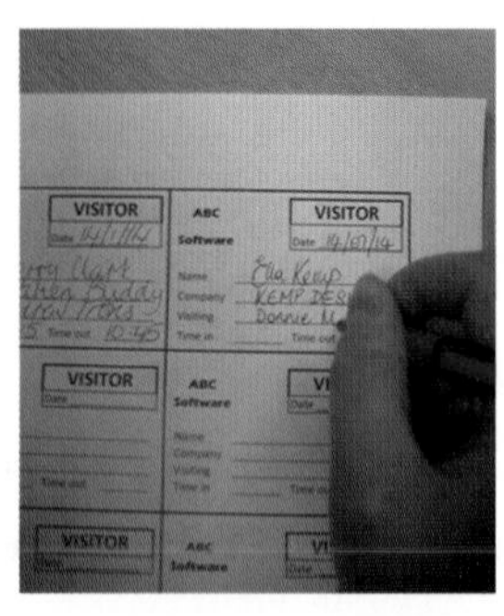

- Any visitor should enter by the main entrance, which should be well signposted to avoid any confusion.
- Once the purpose of the visit is established, the visitor should sign in and collect a visitor badge. This allows the organisation to have a record of the time and purpose of the visit and is part of the safety procedure of most organisations.
- The visitor should wait to be escorted to wherever their appointment is.
- At the end of the visit, the visitor should return the visitor badge and sign out, usually including the time of departure.

Property

Most organisations spend a lot of money on property and equipment. It is important to prevent theft or damage of these expensive items and so security measures are put in place to protect them.

Security measure	Employee	Organisation
Locked doors	must ensure that rooms are locked when leaving	must provide employees with keys of rooms they need to access
Keypad/combination locks	must remember any codes required to access locked areas	must install keypads and ensure all staff are aware of codes – where necessary
	must not prop open doors	codes should be regularly changed to avoid misuse
Fingerprint recognition	must supply their fingerprint to the organisation	must organise the recording of fingerprints of all authorised staff
Swipe card	issued with a plastic card which is programmed to open the door when swiped	must ensure the security code is up to date on the swipe card
	must keep all swipe cards secure	
CCTV/Security staff	may be employed as security staff to monitor the cameras and patrol the building	can install cameras around the building which can see in and around the building recordings can be made if required

Figure 1.1 Keypad

Figure 1.2 Fingerprint recognition

Figure 1.3 Swipe card

Figure 1.4 CCTV

Information

Businesses cannot function without information (**data**). The way information is stored has changed very much with advances in computer technology. Most organisations store important information in an electronic format.

Type of information	Where/How stored
Contacts: clients, suppliers, advertisers	Names, addresses, phone numbers, email addresses all need to be carefully stored so that they can be found when required. This type of information is usually stored electronically in a database, which can be easily updated and searched for quick and easy access *OR* the information can be stored in email software in a contacts list.
Business documents	Letters, emails, invoices, statements, booking forms need to be filed for reference purposes. This type of information is usually stored electronically as a word-processing document or a spreadsheet and saved in folders on a network. This type of storage of information is easily recalled, edited, reprinted or sent in the post or as an attachment to an email.

Type of information	Where/How stored
Recordings/blogs/ discussion forums	A lot of business takes place electronically. This type of information is usually stored electronically as sound and video files. It can therefore be referred to easily, copied or sent as an attachment to an email.

Security of information

A business can use several methods to restrict who can access information and keep the ICT software secure.

The most common method of restricting access to information is of course the use of individual usernames and **passwords** on computers or networks.

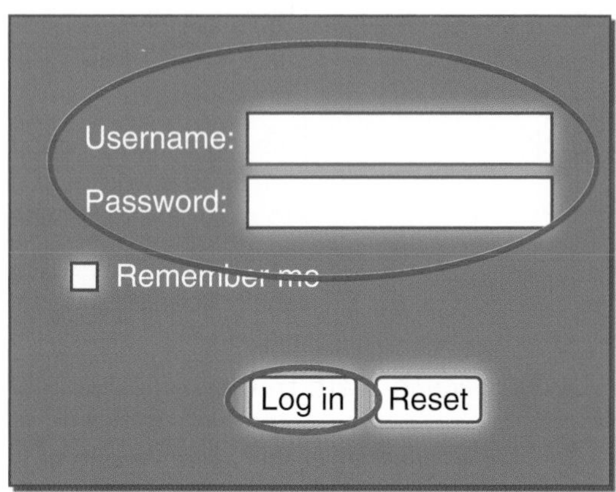

An effective password should contain a random mixture of letters and numbers so that it is more difficult to guess.

There are some **Dos** and **Don'ts** on the proper use of passwords:

Do	Don't
memorise your password	write your password on a sticky note and attach it to your monitor or leave it on your workstation
use a mixture of letters and numbers or unusual capitalisation	use your own name or something else that can be easily guessed at
change your password regularly	share your password with other people

Don't forget about confidential data on the desktop when you leave your workstation. Activate a password-protected screensaver when leaving a computer with documents open on the desktop or close all documents and log off or shut down the computer.

Back-ups

It is essential that important information is backed up (copied to another location) regularly to make sure that if it is corrupted or lost, it can be replaced with the most up-to-date version available. Most organisations have a procedure which automatically backs up the network at the end of every working day. **Back-up** copies are usually stored separately, in case something goes wrong.

Anti-virus software

A virus is a computer program which is created to interfere with the working of computer systems and networks. A virus can be easily spread from one system to another; one of the most common methods of spreading a virus is by email. It is important that anti-virus software is installed to run automatically to clean the system – known as scanning – and also that this software is updated regularly.

Data Protection Act 1998

The Act covers any data about a living and identifiable individual. Individuals can be identified by their name, address, telephone number or email address. The Act applies only to data which is held, or intended to be held, on computers or held in a 'relevant filing system'. In some cases even a paper address book can be classified as a 'relevant filing system', for example diaries used to support commercial activities such as a salesperson's diary. Diaries kept for personal use are not covered under this act.

Data protection principles

The principles state that **personal data** must:

1. be collected and processed fairly and lawfully
2. be obtained only for a specified purpose, and not be further processed
3. be adequate, relevant and not excessive in relation to the purpose for which it is processed
4. be accurate and, where necessary, kept up to date
5. not be processed for any purpose nor be kept for longer than is necessary
6. be protected by proper security methods.

The Act also states that:

7. individuals must be able to access the data held about themselves
8. personal data cannot be transferred outwith the European Union.

National 4 & 5 task

Use the internet to find more information about the Data Protection Act using the Scottish Government website **www.scotland.gov.uk**. Bookmark this site for future reference.

Unit 1

Administrative Practices

Chapter 2

Organising and supporting events

By the end of this chapter you will be able to demonstrate an understanding of:

- ✓ the different types of events that Administrative Assistants have to organise
- ✓ the documents that are used to plan and support events
- ✓ the follow-up tasks that are carried out.

An event is a gathering of people to discuss ideas, make decisions and share information. Successful events are well organised; this requires careful planning and preparation before the event takes place and includes making sure everything is finalised after the event.

Type of event	
Meeting	Meetings are often formal events held at regular intervals where groups come together to discuss topics. The meeting is run by one person: the chairperson. The Admin Assistant will help the chairperson prepare for the meeting by creating an agenda, booking a room and inviting **delegates** to attend.
Presentation	Organisations often hold presentations where people are invited to speak to groups. This could be a training event for staff or simply to pass on important information to delegates. The Admin Assistant will support the event by booking a venue, inviting delegates and speakers and updating slides in a presentation for the speaker.
Interview	Interviews are often held when new staff are required in the organisation. The Admin Assistant will create a database of all the applicants' details and send letters to them to invite them to the interview. They will book a room for the interviews to take place in and place notices outside the room so the interviews aren't disturbed on the day.
Fundraiser	Fundraisers are held to raise money for charities. Admin Assistants will help support the event by creating posters to advertise it and writing to sponsors to ask for donations of prizes.

Type of event	
Promotional event/ launch	Organisations need to promote what they are doing, especially when they are about to start selling something new. Admin Assistants will support these types of events by contacting customers to invite them along. They will create name badges to help people get to know each other at the event more easily.
Business trip	Staff often have to travel on business, to visit customers or suppliers or to visit another branch of the company. The Admin Assistant will help support the business trip by organising travel and accommodation and preparing an itinerary to summarise what will be happening on the trip (for example train times, times of meetings).

Plan

- Before the event takes place, it is important to plan ahead. Let people know about the event and make any bookings or reservations.

Planning tasks

Planning for any event should start as early as possible. For smaller-scale events, planning should start at least two weeks before the event takes place. For larger-scale events, where there are lots of people attending and bookings that need to be made, planning will have to start at least two months in advance.

If planning does not take place far enough in advance, it may be difficult to book venues (as they may be fully booked) and delegates may not be able to attend at short notice and so there will be a low turnout.

Creating a to-do list or action plan to help identify the tasks that need to be done before the event, the order they need to be done in and when they need to be done by, is a simple but very important document to prepare to make sure nothing is forgotten.

To-do list

✓ Select date
✓ Find and book venue
✓ Invite delegates
✓ Photocopy hand-outs
✓ Make name badges

Step 1: date and time

The first step in the planning process is to find a suitable date and time for the event. This will have to be discussed with the event organiser, as they may already have a date in mind.

It may be necessary to find out from delegates who need to attend when they are available, so that the best date can be chosen. Electronic diaries often have a feature that allows other users to look at their calendars and see when they may be available. There are also online tools that can be used to help select dates for meetings, such as **www.doodle.com**, where delegates can select, from a range of dates given, which ones they can and cannot make. The date that suits the most people can then be selected.

STAFF MEETING

Edit your poll | 6 |

Where: Conference Room

6 participants	November Mon 11 09:00	Mon 11 14:00	Tue 12 09:00	Tue 12 14:00	Wed 13 09:00	Wed 13 14:00	Thu 14 09:00	Thu 14 14:00	Fri 15 09:00	Fri 15 14:00
Delegate 1	✓			✓			✓	✓	✓	
Delegate 2	✓	✓			✓	✓	✓	✓	✓	✓
Delegate 3			✓	✓		✓	✓		✓	
Delegate 4	✓	✓			✓	✓			✓	
Delegate 5	✓		✓		✓		✓		✓	
Delegate 6										
Your name	◎	◎	◎	◎	◎	◎	◎	◎	◎	◎
	4	2	2	2	3	3	4	2	5	1

Most popular date: Friday, 15 November 09:00 | Close poll▾

Step 2: booking a venue and resources

A suitable place to hold the event will be needed – it might be possible to use a meeting room in the organisation (internal), but depending on the number of people attending it might be necessary to use an external venue, like a hotel or conference venue. Usually a booking request form is completed to book a venue and this form will also include requests for any equipment (such as data projectors, WiFi access, flip charts) and catering requirements that might be needed during the event. It is important to note down any special requirements, particularly delegates' dietary requirements.

Booking Request Form

Contact name:			
Contact details:			
Name of event:			
Date of event:			
Start time:		Finish time:	
Number of delegates:			
Room layout:			
Equipment required:			
Catering and refreshments:			
Special requests:			

Room layouts

When completing the booking form, it is important to highlight how the room is to be laid out. Venues will be happy to work with the organiser to lay out the room in the way that will suit the event. For more complicated ideas, a drawing or diagram of the layout required should be submitted.

Boardroom This type of layout is popular in events such as meetings with smaller numbers, where everyone must be involved in the same discussion.	

Cabaret This type of layout is often used in larger events where there are to be group discussions. It might be used during a staff training event, where short presentations are given and then groups have to discuss ideas and issues after the presentation is complete.	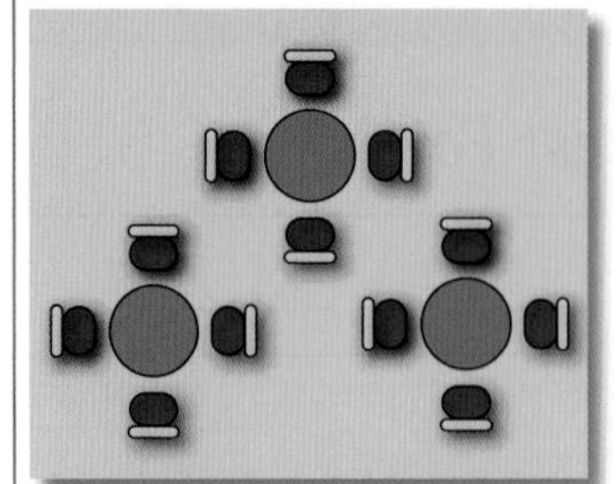
Horseshoe This layout style is often used for small meetings or discussion groups where there is a speaker or presentation.	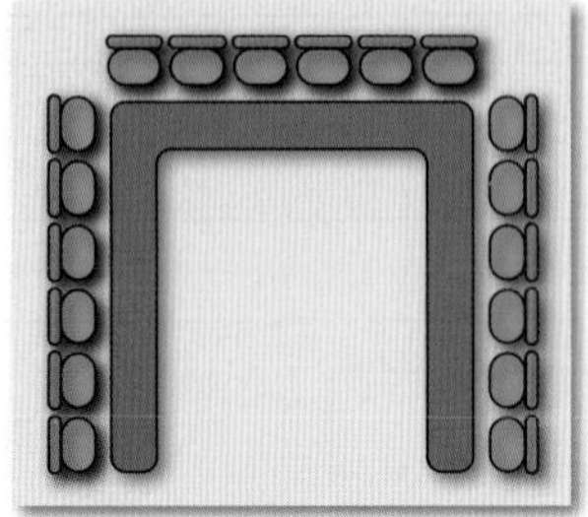
Theatre This style of layout is used when delegates attending an event are acting as an audience. They are there to listen to a speaker or presentation and there will be no need for them to speak or discuss while listening.	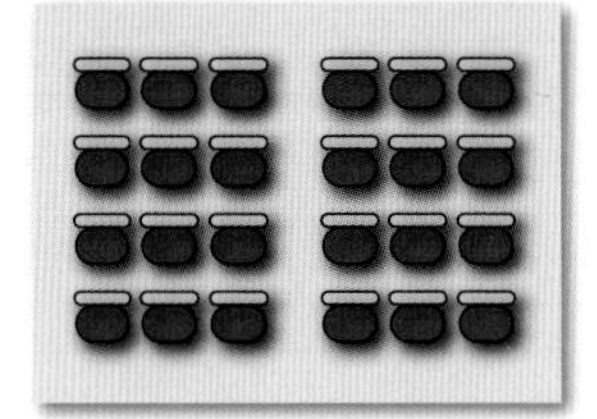

Common forms of room layout

Step 3: inviting delegates

Once the date and time have been agreed and the venue has been confirmed, it is important to alert the delegates to the chosen date, time and venue so that they can make a note in their diaries. In this early email, you will ask delegates to confirm their attendance and ask if they have any special requests or requirements.

Delegates may have dietary requirements or disabilities that need to be taken into account when planning the event – you will have to alert the appropriate staff so that arrangements can be made.

Delegates may also require travel or accommodation arranged for them if they have a long journey to get to the event.

Step 4: travel and accommodation

When delegates request travel or accommodation, the Admin Assistant is required to book it. A travel and accommodation request form is completed by the traveller, giving details of their requirements. This means that the information needed to make the booking is all in one place.

Travel And Accommodation Request Form

Title [ ] First name [ ] Surname [ ]

Reason for request:

Travel

Method of travel requested:

Air ☐ Coach ☐ Ferry ☐ Rail ☐

Departing from: [ ] Arriving at: [ ]

Date of outbound journey: [ ] Date of return journey: [ ]

Time of outbound journey: [ ] Time of return journey: [ ]

Accommodation

Date of arrival: [ ] Number of nights: [ ]

Location of accommodation: [ ]

Most organisations have a policy on how travel and accommodation requests should be dealt with, and the Admin Assistant must take into account the requests of the traveller, whilst making sure they follow company policy (see right).

Once bookings are made, a confirmation is received detailing what has been booked. This must be checked and then sent to the traveller.

It is important to keep a copy of the booking confirmation. If there is a problem with the booking this is the only proof you have of what was booked.

Company Travel and Accommodation Policy

- ☐ Accommodation can only be booked when the traveller lives more than 50 miles away from the venue.
- ☐ A maximum of £100 per person per night can be spent on accommodation.
- ☐ First class travel is not allowed at any time.

National 4 & 5 task

You have received the following travel and accommodation request form which you need to process. Use the internet to find suitable train times and accommodation for Laura.

Accommodation budget:
£100

Travel And Accommodation Request Form

Title: Miss | First name: Laura | Surname: Hamilton

Reason for request:
Training event in Glasgow, travelling from Dumfries.

Travel

Method of travel requested:

Air ☐ Coach ☐ Ferry ☐ Rail ☑

Departing from:	Dumfries	Arriving at:	Glasgow
Date of outbound journey:	next Thursday	Date of return journey:	next Friday
Time of outbound journey:	15:00	Time of return journey:	18:00

Accommodation

Date of arrival:	next Thursday	Number of nights:	one
Location of accommodation:	Glasgow City Centre, as close to the station as possible		

Prepare

- Prepare any documents that are needed to support the event.

There are many documents that you might be asked to produce or **edit**, making use of your IT skills, to support the event.

Name badges	Useful at events where there are lots of people who haven't met before.
Attendance registers	To confirm who has made it to the event and who hasn't. Also important in the event of a fire evacuation.
Signs and notices	During an interview, a sign on the door saying 'DO NOT DISTURB – INTERVIEW IN PROGRESS' would be required. At a large event, direction signs could be useful to direct delegates to the correct room.
Maps	Maps or directions to the venue where the event is being held could be issued to delegates in advance.
Letters	For formal events, a letter may be sent to provide more details to delegates or other guests. *See Chapter 5.*
Database	A record of all delegates can be made in a database. It may also be useful to record who has confirmed attendance, so reminders can be sent to those who still have to get back to you. *See Chapter 3.*
Spreadsheet	A record of all the costs of the event can be made in a spreadsheet. This helps keep track of the **budget** and makes sure there is not an overspend. *See Chapter 4.*
Presentation	If an event has a speaker, it may be necessary to prepare a presentation for them to use. Presentations could also be used in the reception area to give information about the event, while people are waiting. *See Chapter 7.*

Documents used at events

Some events have very specific documents that must always be produced.

Meetings require an **agenda** which provides a list of items that will be discussed at the meeting. **Minutes**, which provide a record of what was discussed during the meeting, must be taken. The minutes from the previous meeting are always provided at the next meeting.

The meeting of the Social Committee will take place in the Boardroom at 1700 hours on 20 October.

AGENDA

1) Attendance and apologies for absence
2) Minutes of last meeting
3) Matters arising
4) Correspondence
5) Proposal for staff outing
6) Funding
7) Any other business
8) Date of next meeting

A Bradley
Secretary

MINUTES of the Social Committee meeting which took place in the Boardroom at 1700 hours on 20 October.

PRESENT: A McKeown (Chair), A Boyle, A M Chalmers, K Lyons, M Mallon, A Bradley (Secretary)

APOLOGIES FOR ABSENCE: A Stephenson

MINUTES OF LAST MEETING

The minutes of the last meeting were accepted and approved.

MATTERS ARISING

There were no matters arising from the last meeting

CORRESPONDENCE

1) The Secretary read a letter from the Director regarding the use of the Canteen for future social events.
2) The Chairman informed the meeting of the receipt of a licence for the Christmas party.

PROPOSAL FOR STAFF OUTING

After a general discussion, it was decided that the staff should be balloted to find their preferences for the format of the Christmas party before any final decision be made.

FUNDING

Funding will be provided from the subscriptions paid by the staff. It was decided that this will be discussed in greater detail at the next meeting.

ANY OTHER BUSINESS

There was no other business to discuss.

DATE OF NEXT MEETING

The next meeting will be held on the first Friday of next month.

A McKeown
Chair

ITINERARY

Glasgow Branch Manager's trip to London Head Office
Wednesday 6th July – Thursday 7th July

Wednesday 6 July

0900 hours	Train departs Glasgow Central Station
1330 hours	Train arrives at London Euston Station
1400 hours	Check in at Travelodge, Drury Lane

Thursday 7 July

1000 hours	Meeting with Customer Services Manager at Head Office
1300 hours	Lunch
1400 hours	Meeting with Human Resources Manager at Head Office
1800 hours	Train departs London Euston Station
2230 hours	Train arrives at Glasgow Central Station

For a business trip, an itinerary is required. This provides a breakdown of what will happen on the trip in time order.

National 4 & 5 task

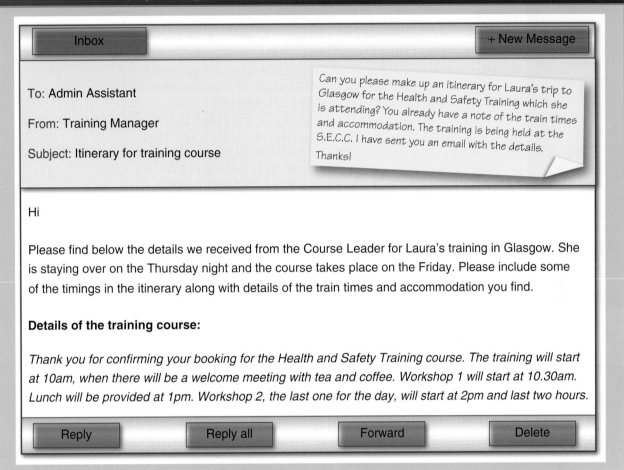

Inbox

+ New Message

To: Admin Assistant

From: Training Manager

Subject: Itinerary for training course

Can you please make up an itinerary for Laura's trip to Glasgow for the Health and Safety Training which she is attending? You already have a note of the train times and accommodation. The training is being held at the S.E.C.C. I have sent you an email with the details.

Thanks!

Hi

Please find below the details we received from the Course Leader for Laura's training in Glasgow. She is staying over on the Thursday night and the course takes place on the Friday. Please include some of the timings in the itinerary along with details of the train times and accommodation you find.

Details of the training course:

Thank you for confirming your booking for the Health and Safety Training course. The training will start at 10am, when there will be a welcome meeting with tea and coffee. Workshop 1 will start at 10.30am. Lunch will be provided at 1pm. Workshop 2, the last one for the day, will start at 2pm and last two hours.

Reply | Reply all | Forward | Delete

Follow up

- When the event is finished, complete any tasks that are needed, for example updating documents, sending out thank you messages.

When the event is finished there may be a number of tasks that have to be completed by the Admin Assistant to bring everything to a close. These tasks will vary depending on the type of event and who was involved.

Update spreadsheet/ database files	Once all the invoices have been received from the event, it may be necessary to update the budget with the actual figures and check if the budget was kept to. The database can be updated with details of who attended the event and who didn't make it.
Thank you messages	Thank you letters or emails may be sent out to delegates or any visiting speakers from the organisation.

Updates	After an event, organisations like to promote what happened and the outcomes of the event. After a fundraiser, for example, it is good to hear how much was raised and what the money will be used for. The Admin Assistant may be asked to insert an article into a newsletter or update the company website with a message or article about the event from the organiser.
Minutes	Meetings require minutes to be taken to record what was discussed and what needs to be done. The Admin Assistant is often required to type these up and email them to everyone who attended.
Process expenses	If the event involved travelling, staff and delegates are often able to claim back any expenses for fuel, car parking, train tickets, etc. The Admin Assistant will receive expenses claim forms and receipts and check all the details are correct. He or she has to make sure that any rules about what can or cannot be claimed, contained in policy documents, have been adhered to.
Feedback forms	After most events, organisers want to get feedback from delegates on how well it was organised and whether the venue was suitable and the speakers useful and interesting. The Admin Assistant will create the form and send it out to the delegates. Organisations often use online survey websites such as **www.surveymonkey.com** to create questionnaires that they can email to the delegates for feedback.

Follow-up tasks after an event

National 4 & 5 task

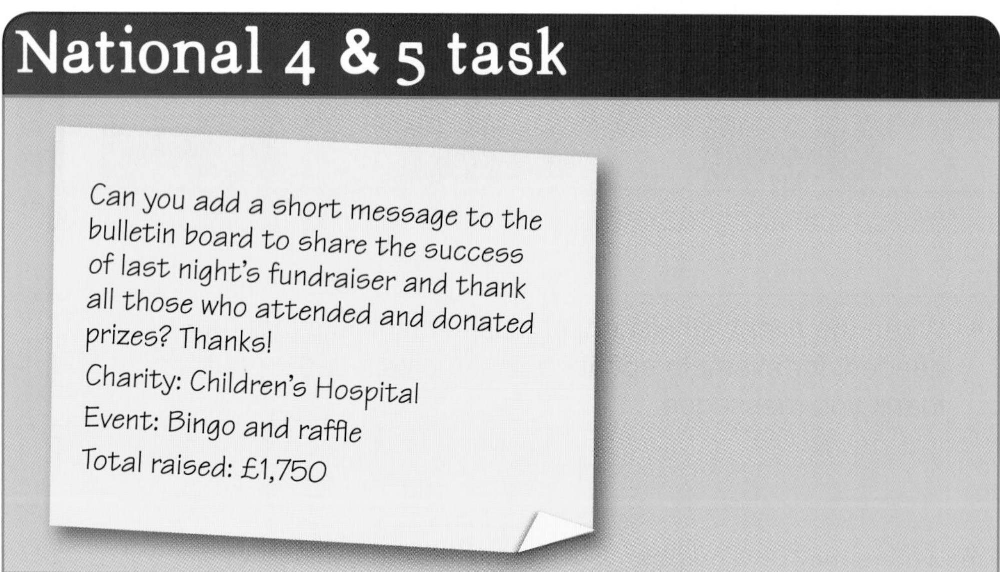

Can you add a short message to the bulletin board to share the success of last night's fundraiser and thank all those who attended and donated prizes? Thanks!
Charity: Children's Hospital
Event: Bingo and raffle
Total raised: £1,750

National 5 task

Please can you check these expense claims and add the correct information to the expenses spreadsheet? Please amend any errors as you do this.

Travel Expenses Policy

- Mileage for fuel is 45p per mile. No receipt is required for claims for fuel.
- Receipts for all other expenses must be attached to the claim or the claim will be rejected.
- Travel by rail or air can only be claimed for standard/economy class.
- Accommodation costs cannot be claimed back. Accommodation must be booked through our booking agent, who will bill the company directly.
- Subsistence claims (lunch, evening meals, snacks) can be made. A maximum of £5 per day for lunch and £20 per day for evening meals can be claimed back.

Expenses Claim Form

Name: *Jay young*

Department: *Sales*

Date	Detail	Amount
1 January	*Fuel – 50 miles @ 45p/mile*	*£22.00*
1 January	*Lunch*	*£ 6.75*
TOTAL		*£28.75*

Snack Bar

Meal Deal £6.75

Total £6.75
CASH £10.00

Change £3.25

Thank you!

Speedy Train **COMPANY**

Class	Ticket Type	Adult/Child
STD	Return	ONE/NIL

Date 19-Oct-2013

From GLASGOW CEN/QST
To STIRLING
Cost £17.50

STC

The CENTRAL Hotel

Epney Street
Stirling
Stirlingshire
FK6 3DV

Guest name: Danny Brown Arrival date: 14 May Departure date: 15 May	
Room no.: 105	
Room cost:	£75.00
No other charges incurred.	
TOTAL DUE:	£75.00
Credit Card	£75.00

Paid in full.

We hope you enjoyed your stay!

Expenses Claim Form

Name: *Danny Brown*

Department: *Finance*

Date	Detail	Amount
14may	*Accommodation*	*£ 75.00*
14may	*Train ticket (return)*	*£ 17.50*
14may	*Fuel – 20 miles @ 50p/mile*	*£ 10.00*
15may	*Car parking at Train Station*	*£ 8.00*
TOTAL		*£117.50*

IT Solutions for Administrators

Chapter 3

Use of spreadsheet applications to support admin tasks

By the end of this chapter you will:

- ✓ understand the purpose and uses of spreadsheets within organisations
- ✓ develop skills in creating and editing spreadsheets
- ✓ develop skills in using the functions and formulae of spreadsheets to manage and manipulate information.

Organisations collect lots of information and often this may be in the form of numbers. A spreadsheet is a software application used to store, manage and analyse this type of information. Examples of information that might be recorded in a spreadsheet include:

- records of sales figures
- details of employee wages to be paid out
- budgets to estimate how money can be spent (for example on redecorating a store).

Working with numerical information often means that calculations have to be completed to work out the total amount of money that has been made from sales, how much money should be paid to employees each week or whether the organisation has spent too much.

The same types of calculations are likely to be carried out again and again on this information. A spreadsheet can be created to complete these calculations automatically when **data** is entered. In a spreadsheet, these automatic calculations are set up by entering **formulae**.

A number of features can also be used to manipulate and analyse this information, including sorting the information and creating charts.

First let us have a look at a blank spreadsheet and its features:

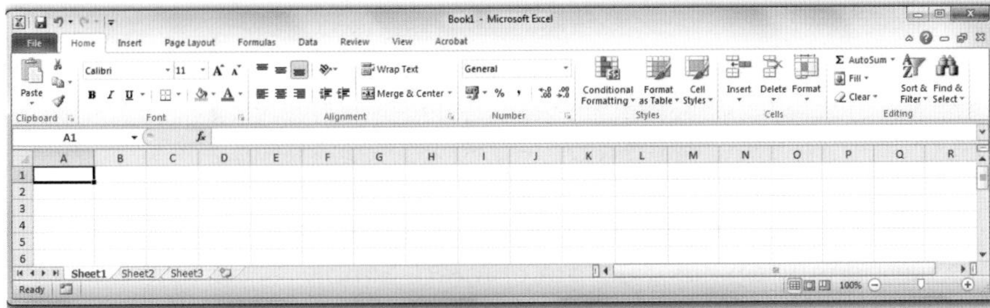

Open a new blank spreadsheet worksheet and before you do anything else save it, using the filename **Staff Wages**.

Cells

A spreadsheet is made up of a number of boxes, called 'cells'. Each cell has a name, a **cell reference**, which is made up of the column letter and row number of the cell.

If you look at the example above, you will see that we are clicked into the cell at the top left hand corner. It is in column A and row 1 – making the cell reference A1. Excel® helps make it easier to identify the cell reference by highlighting, in colour, the column and row that we are clicked in and by telling us the cell reference in the white box just above column A.

When you are working with a spreadsheet, click in different cells and watch the cell reference change.

i

It is very important that you understand how cell references are made up as you will be working with them a lot as you work through this chapter.

Entering data, editing and formatting

Using the blank spreadsheet you have just saved, enter the information in Figure 3.1 into the worksheet, copying it exactly.

	A	B	C	D
1	**Week beginning**	**Number of hours**	**Rate per hour**	**Total**
2	05/08/2013	10	6.75	
3	12/08/2013	12	6.75	
4	19/08/2013	14	6.75	
5	26/08/2013	12	6.75	
6	02/09/2013	12	6.75	
7	09/09/2013	14	6.75	
8	16/09/2013	25	6.75	

Figure 3.1

When data has been entered into a cell, sometimes the column width is not big enough and some of the data is cut off (truncated). It is important to check back over anything you have entered to make sure everything is visible.

If you notice ###### has appeared in a column, this is because a column is not wide enough. This sometimes happens when numbers are entered. Simply increasing the column width brings back the data you entered. Let's have a look at this problem in Figure 3.2.

Here there seems to be a problem with column A. The heading is truncated and the numbers entered into the column are too big to be seen.

There are two ways to solve this problem; you should try both and use the method you prefer.

Method 1

- Take your pointer and hover between the two columns (A and B in this example). Your pointer will change into a vertical line with two arrows pointing out (look at Figure 3.2, showing what your pointer will change to – it has been circled it to make it easier to spot).
- As soon as your pointer has changed, click with the left mouse button, hold and drag to the right – this will let you increase the column to the width you want.

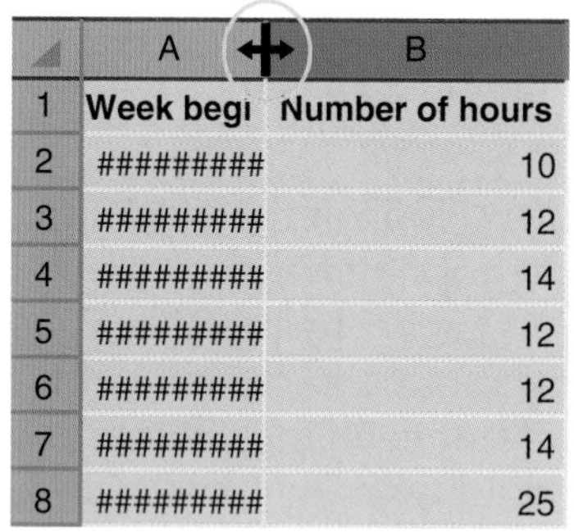

	A	B
1	Week begi	Number of hours
2	#########	10
3	#########	12
4	#########	14
5	#########	12
6	#########	12
7	#########	14
8	#########	25

Figure 3.2

Method 2

- In the same way as the first method, take your pointer and hover between the two columns (A and B in this example).
- When your pointer has changed, this time double-click the left mouse button and the spreadsheet will change the column to the best size to fit the data for you.

All the data is now visible (Figure 3.3).

	A	B
1	Week beginning	Number of hours
2	05/08/2013	10
3	12/08/2013	12
4	19/08/2013	14
5	26/08/2013	12
6	02/09/2013	12
7	09/09/2013	14
8	16/09/2013	25

Figure 3.3

Wrapping text

It is often useful, mainly to save space, to wrap text – this is where the words are made to stack up under each other rather than continuing on one line. You can see below what unwrapped and wrapped text looks like in Figures 3.4 and 3.5 respectively.

	A	B	C	D
1	Week beginning	Number of hours	Rate per hour	Total
2	05/08/2013	10	6.75	
3	12/08/2013	12	6.75	
4	19/08/2013	14	6.75	
5	26/08/2013	12	6.75	
6	02/09/2013	12	6.75	
7	09/09/2013	14	6.75	
8	16/09/2013	25	6.75	

Figure 3.4

	A	B	C	D
1	Week beginning	Number of hours	Rate per hour	Total
2	05/08/2013	10	6.75	
3	12/08/2013	12	6.75	
4	19/08/2013	14	6.75	
5	26/08/2013	12	6.75	
6	02/09/2013	12	6.75	
7	09/09/2013	14	6.75	
8	16/09/2013	25	6.75	

Figure 3.5

- So to wrap the headings, highlight the cells that you want to wrap and then click 'Wrap Text'.

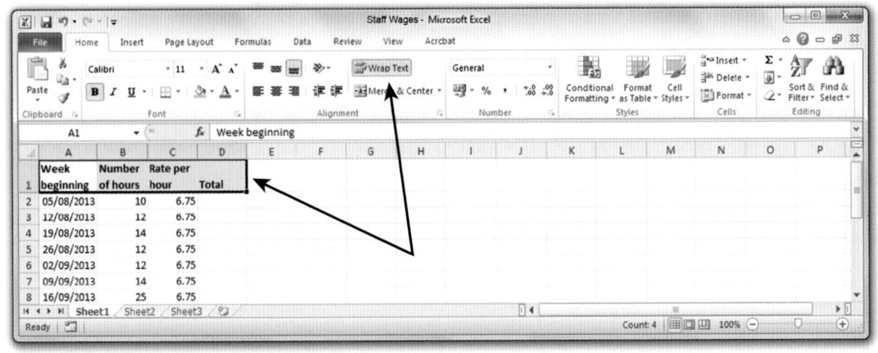

Figure 3.6

Sometimes you have to reduce the size of the column and increase the size of the row, if the headings don't appear to have wrapped.

In Figure 3.6, only the headings have been wrapped, but text can be wrapped in any cell within the spreadsheet.

Formatting cells

One of the important checks for a spreadsheet is to make sure that all the data that has been entered is correct, including any symbols. The easiest way to do this is to type the symbols as you enter the data. Sometimes, data may have already been entered into a spreadsheet and you may be asked to make a range of numbers or a particular row or column show as currency or percentage.

Rather than type these individual symbols into each cell, which if there are a lot could take a while and you might miss out one by accident, the fastest way is to get the spreadsheet to add these symbols for you:

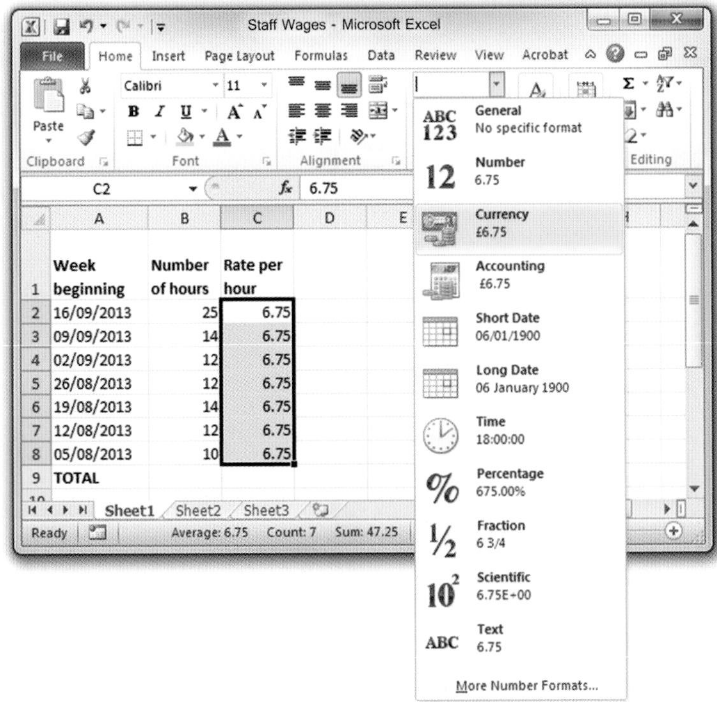

- Highlight the cells you want to format.
- From the Home ribbon, click the dropdown menu in the number section.
- You will be presented with a list of choices; the most frequently used ones are displayed. In this example we have highlighted Rate per hour, so we will select Currency and the spreadsheet will add a £ sign to all the numbers we selected.

It is important to check the following when entering data into a spreadsheet:

- is the data being inserted in the correct place (correct row and column)?
- is all the data visible once entered?
- is it **formatted** correctly and consistently in the same font and size as all the other data, and are any symbols (such as £, %, decimal points) all present?

Alignment

We are often asked to change the position of data within a cell (cell alignment). This can simply be to centre or right align, for example:

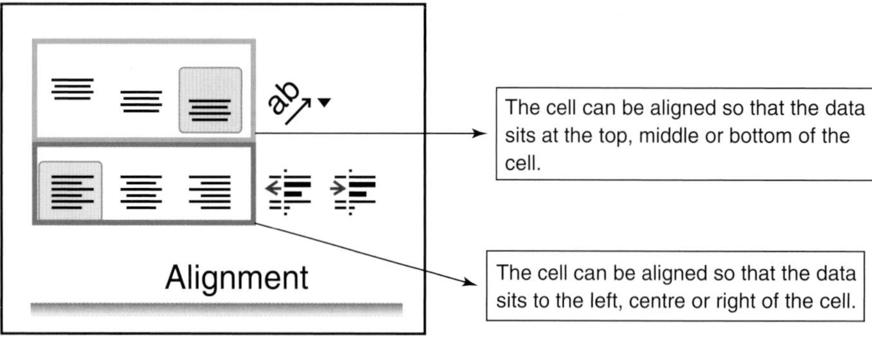

Alignment
The cell can be aligned so that the data sits at the top, middle or bottom of the cell.
The cell can be aligned so that the data sits to the left, centre or right of the cell.

It is also possible to change the angle of the data within a cell:

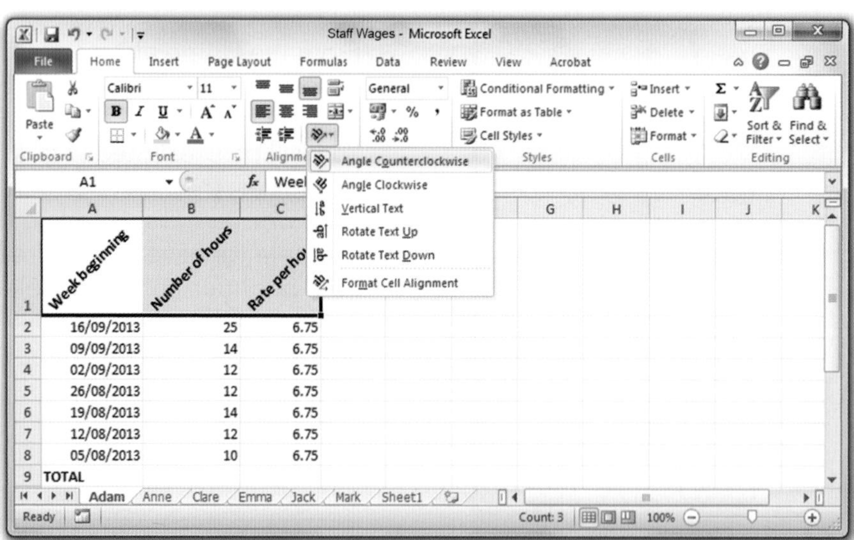

Borders

We are able to add a border to a cell or a range of cells. This is often used to make the data in a cell stand out.

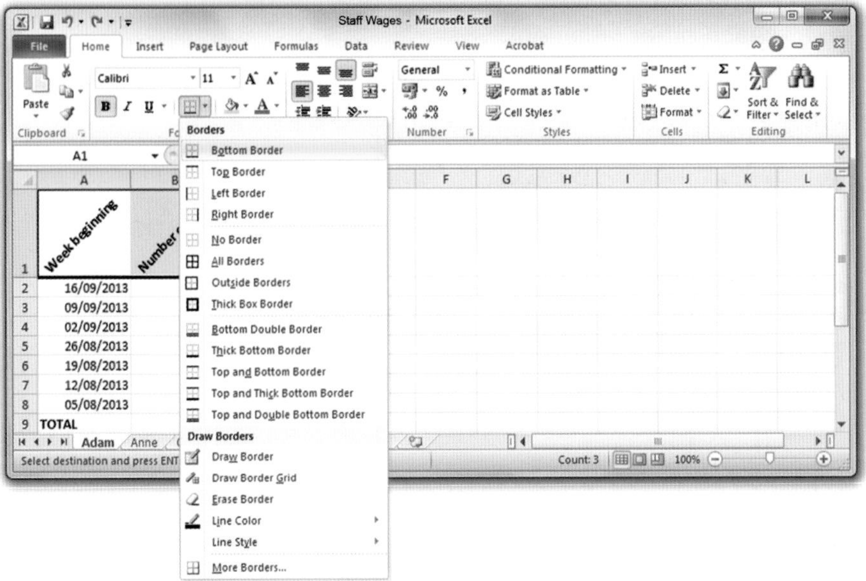

- Highlight the cell(s) that the border is to outline.
- From the Home ribbon, select the Borders menu.
- You will be presented with a list of different options.
- Once you have selected the border you want to use, you can go back into the border menu and change the colour (Line Color menu) or Line Style (thinner or thicker borders or dashed borders).

Shading

Another popular method used to highlight particular cells or simply to improve the appearance of the spreadsheet is to add shading.

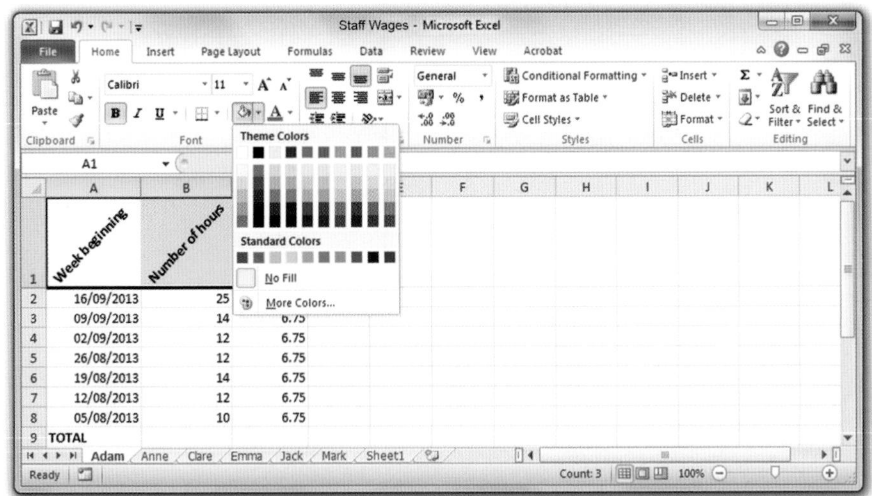

- Highlight the cell(s) you want to shade.
- Using the Home ribbon, click the arrow next to the paint can.
- Select a colour (remember to think carefully about your choice of colour – if it is too dark, the writing will be difficult to see, especially if you want to print the spreadsheet and you have a black and white printer).

Hiding and unhiding columns/rows

Sometimes it is necessary to hide columns/rows in a worksheet and then unhide them when they need to be seen again. You might want to do this if you only want to print out certain pieces of data or if you want to create a chart using rows/columns that are not next to each other (adjacent).

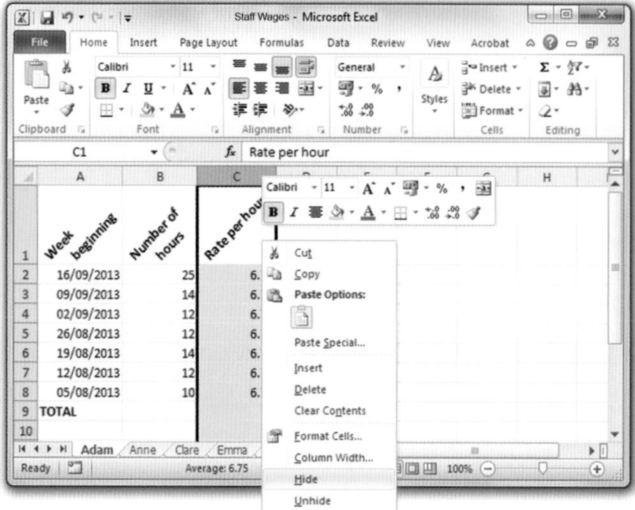

- To hide a column/row, click on the column letter or row number.
- Right-click.
- From the menu, click Hide.

When you want to bring the rows or columns back:

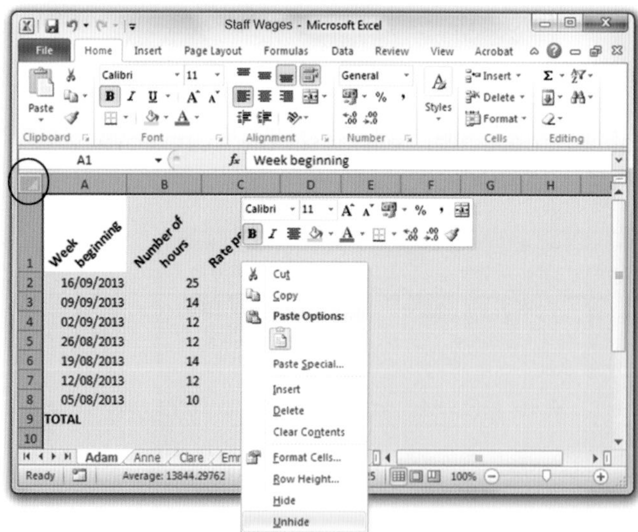

- Click the triangle in the top-left corner of the worksheet: ▢. This will highlight the whole worksheet.
- Right-click anywhere in the worksheet.
- Select Unhide.

Conditional formatting (National 5 only)

It is often quite useful to highlight particular pieces of data in a spreadsheet, especially when there is a lot of data and you are looking for something in particular.

Spreadsheets can be set up to do this automatically. This is called 'conditional formatting'.

In Figure 3.7, we want to see when an employee has worked more than 12 hours.

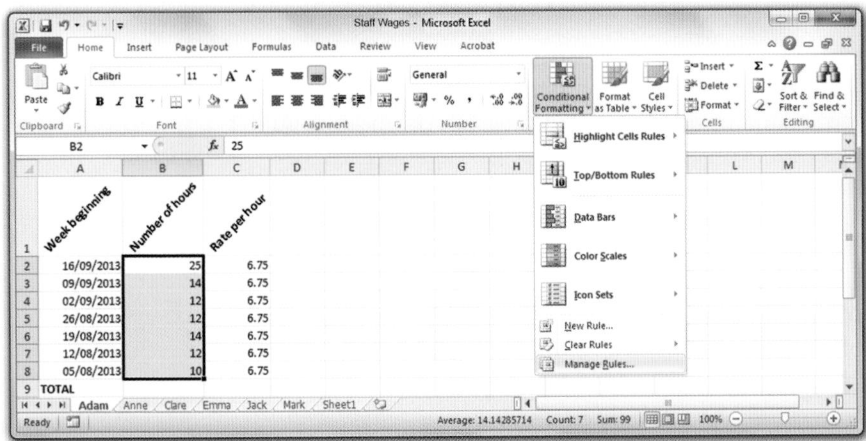

Figure 3.7

- First, highlight the cells that the conditional formatting is to be applied to.
- From the Home ribbon, select the Conditional Formatting menu and then Manage Rules.
- Select New Rule and then from the options listed, select Format only cells that contain.
- Select the criteria 'greater than' from the dropdown list and then type in 12.

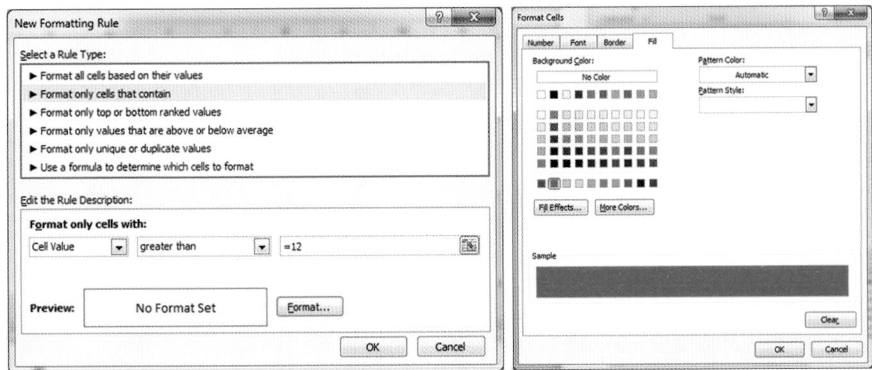

- Then we have to decide what will happen when the spreadsheet finds cells that have values that are greater than 12. In this case, the cells should be shaded red. Click Format and from the Format cells dialog box, select the Fill tab and choose the colour.
- After clicking OK to close all the dialog boxes, you should see that the cells that match the criteria are shaded. If the numbers change, the spreadsheet will update and add or remove shading automatically.

It is possible to add more conditions. Only one condition was used in this example, but more can be added by clicking Add rules.

Changes will only be made to the cell you are clicked in. So if you want to change the font, size or colour of the whole spreadsheet, it's much easier to highlight all the cells you want to change at once, rather than do them one at a time.

Worksheets

A spreadsheet is made up of worksheets. When you have a spreadsheet open, you will see at the bottom of the screen that there are three tabs called Sheet 1, Sheet 2 and Sheet 3. When you click on each of these you will be taken to another blank worksheet.

This is a very useful feature of a spreadsheet as it means you can store lots of similar information in one place. This will make the information easy to access and you will also save space on the network.

If we take the example of staff wages we used earlier, we could make our spreadsheet have a worksheet for each employee. This would mean that the spreadsheet would contain the necessary data about staff wages but we would separate it into different worksheets according to employee. More worksheets can be added – we are not limited to three – and you can even change the name of the tab, that is, the worksheet:

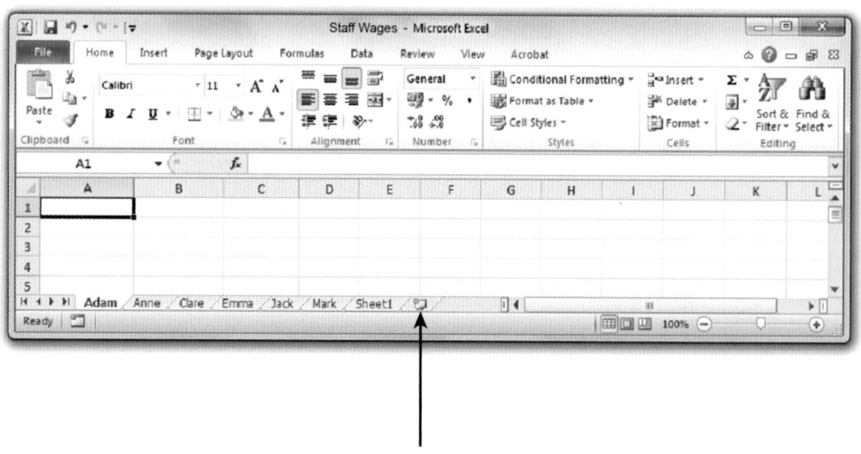

- Add a new worksheet by clicking here.
- Or from the Home ribbon click Insert:

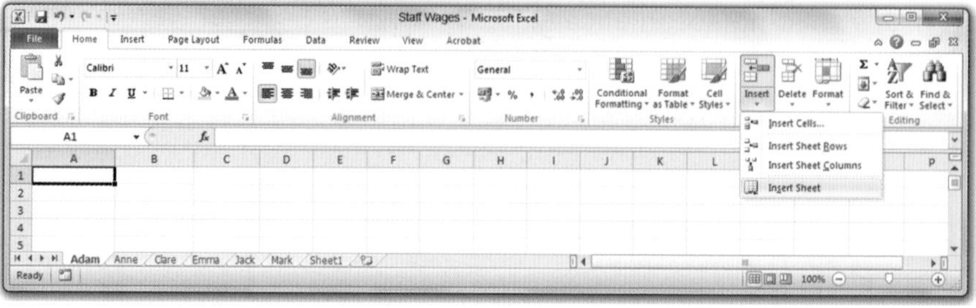

To change the name of the worksheet, right-click on tab you want to rename and select Rename. In your saved spreadsheet, name the first worksheet 'Adam'.

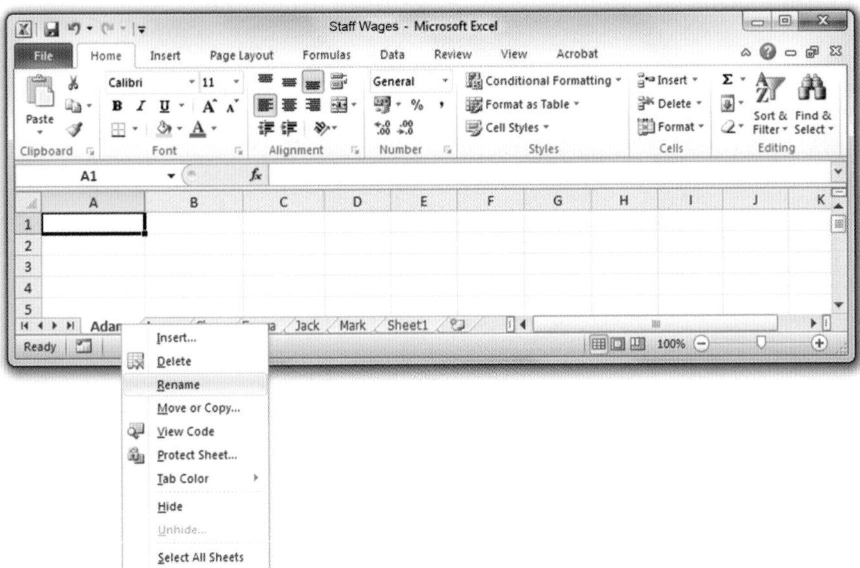

You will also notice that, when you right-click one of the tabs, there are a lot of other options; the ones you will find most useful are:

- delete – this will delete the worksheet that you clicked on
- tab color – you can change the tabs to different colours, which is useful if you have lots of tabs and want to find a particular one quickly.

You can also move the sheets around, if you would prefer them to be in a certain order. They might need to be alphabetical, for instance. The worksheets can be moved by clicking and holding the tab with the left-hand mouse button and then dragging the sheet to where you want to place it.

A handy feature of spreadsheets is the ability to copy the worksheet and its content. A new member of staff might join the organisation, and rather than having to key all the headings and formulae you may have entered already and which will just be the same for the new employee, you can make a copy.

Right-click the tab of the worksheet you want to copy, select Move or Copy and you will be presented with this dialog box:

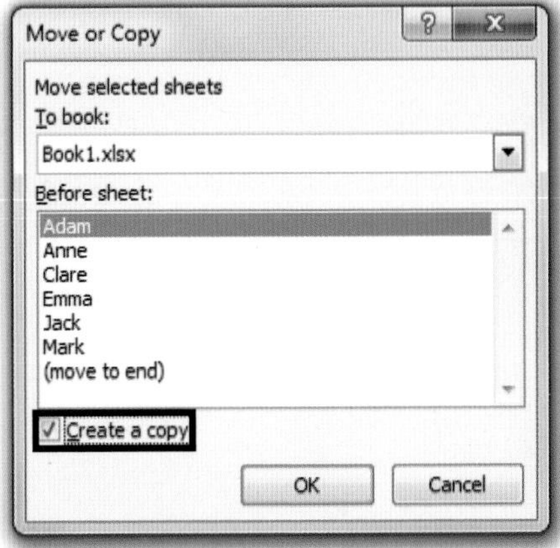

Here you can choose where you want the new copy to go (either before one of the worksheets that is already there or at the end, but you can move it later if you click the wrong one).

Don't forget to tick the box Create a copy and then click OK. The new sheet will be inserted.

A spreadsheet that has a number of worksheets in it is called a 'workbook'.

Formulae

Spreadsheets can complete calculations automatically, once we have entered a formula or function into a cell.

A formula is a code that we enter into a cell. First we need to understand how to make up a basic formula. Let's look at how to add up two numbers using a formula.

Here is a very simple spreadsheet. We want to add the numbers in cells A1 and B2 and for the answer to be shown in cell C1.

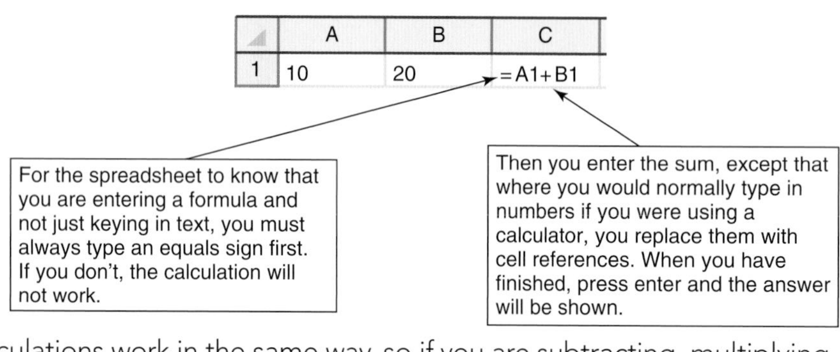

A
B
C
1
10
20
=A1+B1
For the spreadsheet to know that you are entering a formula and not just keying in text, you must always type an equals sign first. If you don't, the calculation will not work.
Then you enter the sum, except that where you would normally type in numbers if you were using a calculator, you replace them with cell references. When you have finished, press enter and the answer will be shown.

All calculations work in the same way, so if you are subtracting, multiplying or dividing, you follow the same process. You have to be careful when multiplying or dividing, as different symbols are used, as shown in Table 3.1.

Maths symbol	Symbol used in Excel®
+	+
-	-
×	*
÷	/

Table 3.1

It's handy to use the numeric keypad, as all these symbols are easy to find there.

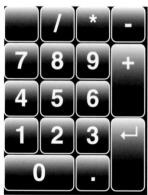

	A	B	C	D
1	1	2	3	4
2	5	6	7	8
3	9	10	11	12
4	13	14	15	16
5	17	18	19	20
6	21	22	23	24
7	25	26	27	28

Figure 3.8

Here are some sums. Using the data in the spreadsheet in Figure 3.8, what formulae would you enter?

For example: 1 + 27 as a formula would be =A1+C7

1. 24 + 14
2. 10 ÷ 2
3. 28 – 19
4. 26 × 7

1. =D6+B4 2. =B3/B1 3. =D7–C5 4. =B7*C2

You don't have to type in the cell references. You can use your mouse and click the cells you want to include in the formula. The only time you need to use the keyboard is to type in the equals sign and the correct maths symbol.

- Going back to our spreadsheet for staff wages, we can enter a formula in column D to calculate how much Adam will be paid each week.
- So for every hour Adam works, he earns £6.75, and to calculate the total for each week we multiply the number of hours per week by the rate per hour.
- You will notice that the formulae are all very similar; the only change is the row number as we move down the different weeks.

	A	B	C	D
1	**Week beginning**	**Number of hours**	**Rate per hour**	**Total**
2	16/09/2013	25	£6.75	=B2*C2
3	19/08/2013	14	£6.75	=B3*C3
4	09/09/2013	14	£6.75	=B4*C4
5	12/08/2013	12	£6.75	=B5*C5
6	26/08/2013	12	£6.75	=B6*C6
7	02/09/2013	12	£6.75	=B7*C7
8	05/08/2013	10	£6.75	=B8*C8

Percentages

Calculations involving percentages are common in spreadsheets due to their use in many aspects of business, for example employees receive a 5% pay rise.

We have to work out the value of the pay rise. This is done by multiplying the amount (B2) by the percentage (5%). Figure 3.9 shows the formula for calculating the pay rise.

Now we have this figure we can either add it (if it's an increase) or subtract it (if it's a decrease, such as a discount) from the original figure. (In this case, we would add it to the current rate.)

	A	B	C
1	**Employee**	**Current Rate**	**Increase**
2	Adam	£6.75	=B2*5%
3	Anne	£8.75	=B3*5%

Figure 3.9

When you are entering formulae that are very similar, the only change being that the next one is in a different row or column, like in the example, you only need to enter the first formula and then the spreadsheet software will copy the formula into the other cells. This is called 'replicating'.

	A	B	C	D
1	**Week beginning**	**Number of hours**	**Rate per hour**	**Total**
2	16/09/2013	25	£6.75	£168.75
3	19/08/2013	14	£6.75	
4	09/09/2013	14	£6.75	
5	12/08/2013	12	£6.75	
6	26/08/2013	12	£6.75	
7	02/09/2013	12	£6.75	
8	05/08/2013	10	£6.75	

Once you have entered the first formula, click back into the cell. Move your pointer to the bottom-right corner of the cell until it changes to a cross and then click, hold and drag down (or double-click the mouse when the pointer changes to a cross).

Functions

Auto-sum

Often we have to add up lots of cells to provide a total. If we were to use the method from earlier, where we enter the cell references, in a large spreadsheet this would be time consuming to complete and we might miss out a cell by mistake. If we wanted to add up all the totals in our Staff Wages spreadsheet to show how much the employee has earned so far we would have to enter =D2+D3+D4+D5+D6+D7+D8. There is a much faster and better way to add up lots of cells. Here's how:

Staff Wages - Microsoft Excel

=SUM(D2:D8)

	A	B	C	D
1	Week beginning	Number of hours	Rate per hour	Total
2	16/09/2013	25	£6.75	£168.75
3	09/09/2013	14	£6.75	£94.50
4	19/08/2013	14	£6.75	£94.50
5	02/09/2013	12	£6.75	£81.00
6	26/08/2013	12	£6.75	£81.00
7	12/08/2013	12	£6.75	£81.00
8	05/08/2013	10	£6.75	£67.50
9	TOTAL			=SUM(D2:D8)

Sum
Average
Count Numbers
Max
Min
More Functions...

Figure 3.10

- Click in the cell where the total is to be displayed (in Figure 3.10 that's cell D9).
- In the Home ribbon click the dropdown arrow next to AutoSum and select Sum. You will notice that some cells have been selected for you and a formula has been entered. Click Enter to accept the formula. If a cell has been highlighted that you don't want to include or one has been missed, you can select the cells you want by highlighting them. Then click Enter.

Spreadsheets have lots of formulae that are pre-entered for us to use. These are called 'functions'. They are found in the function palette:

- In the formula bar click *fx*.
- Select the function you want to use from the list and click OK.
- If the function you want to use is not there, type its name into the search box and click Go.

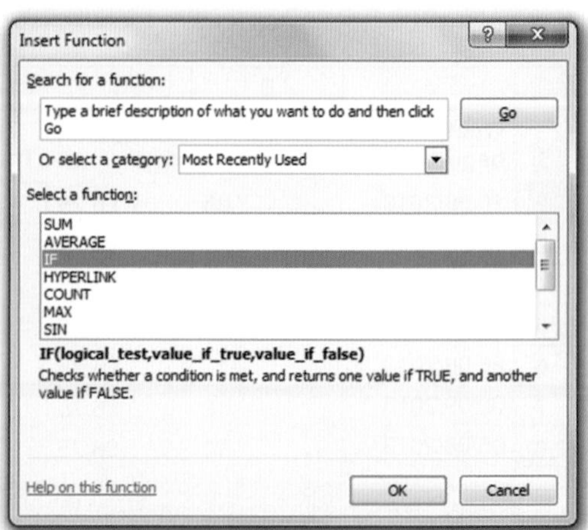

As you start to use the functions, the ones you use most often will appear at the top of the list and you won't need to use the search box as often.

Let's look at some of the functions you are most likely to use and see what they do.

Maximum (Max)	Shows the highest value from the cells that have been highlighted.	**Example data** 14 10 25 12
Minimum (Min)	Shows the lowest value from the cells that have been highlighted.	Max: 25 Min: 10
Average	Calculates the average from the cells that have been highlighted.	Average: 15 CountA: 4
CountA	Counts the number of cells with data that have been highlighted. It will not include blank cells.	CountBLANK: 0 CountIF: if we instructed to count only cells containing values greater than 12 it would return the answer 2
CountBLANK	Counts the number of empty cells from those highlighted.	
CountIF	Counts how many cells, from those that have been highlighted, meet a criteria you have set.	

Using Max, Min, Average, CountA and CountBLANK

Max, Min, Average, CountA and CountBLANK functions are all set up in the same way.

We are going to look at how to calculate the *average* number of hours worked by Adam.

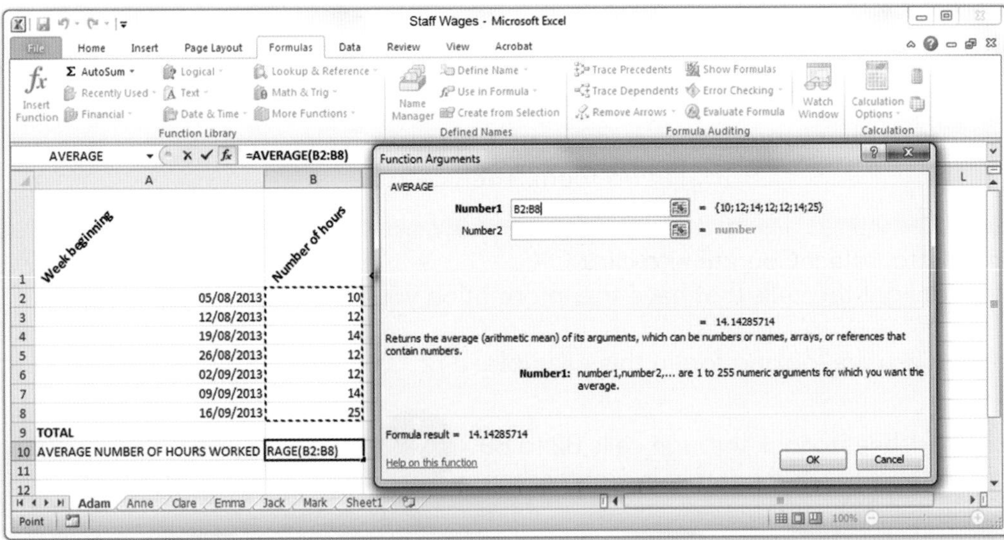

- Click in cell B10.
- In the Formulas ribbon, click **fx** to view the function palette.
- Click Average and click OK.
- A range of cells will be selected and entered into the Number 1 box. If this is what you want click OK, but if not you can highlight the cells you want in the spreadsheet and click OK.
- No information is needed in the Number 2 box.

- Max, Min, CountA and CountBLANK work in exactly the same way as Average and you should follow the same steps as shown on the previous page to set up the function. Practise using the other functions on your spreadsheet.

When you are entering functions and formulae into a spreadsheet, make sure they always have an appropriate heading or label, so anyone looking at the information knows what the figures mean.

Using CountIF (National 5 only)

CountIF is used to tell us how many entries there are in a range that match a criteria. It is set up in a very similar way to the other functions, but there is one main difference. Let's have a look at an example to see how to set it up. Continue to use the file **Staff Wages** to work through the example:

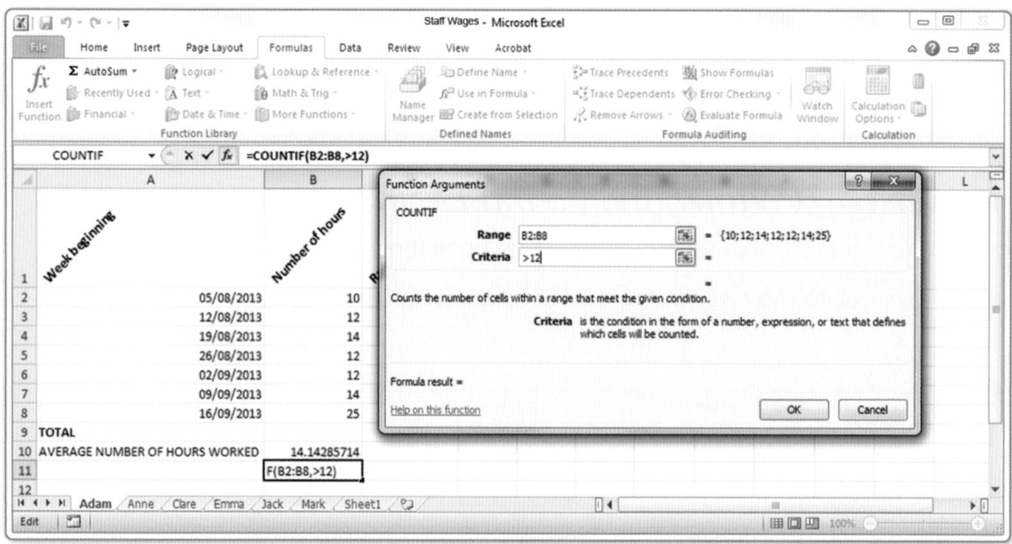

- Click in cell B11.
- From the function palette, select CountIF and click OK.
- Click in Range and highlight the cells that have the information you want to count (B2:B8).
- Type into Criteria what you are looking for; in this example: >12.
- Click OK.

So we have asked the spreadsheet to look through cells B2 to B8 and count how many times there is a number that is greater than 12 and tell us the answer in cell B11.

The CountIF function can count words as well as numbers.

IF statement (National 5 only)

Some entries or calculations in a spreadsheet will depend on other information. We can instruct the spreadsheet to make decisions for us based on criteria that we set.

There are two types of IF statements:

- Where we want a value to be entered
- Where we want a calculation to take place.

Let's look at some examples.

- Set up a new spreadsheet and add the data shown in Figure 3.11.
- Save the file as **Staff Rates**.

	A	B	C
1	**Employee**	**Level**	**Rate per hour**
2	Adam	Junior	
3	Anne	Senior	
4	Clare	Senior	
5	Emma	Junior	
6	Mark	Senior	

Figure 3.11

Employees are paid different rates depending on their level of seniority within the company. Junior staff earn £6.75 per hour and senior staff earn £8.75 per hour.

Rather than enter all this information individually, we can enter a formula into cell C2 and then replicate it to the remaining rows. An IF statement is useful because if there are lots of records it is a quick way of entering information, and if there is a change, for instance someone becomes a senior member of staff, the spreadsheet will automatically change the rate per hour.

- So, with cell C2 highlighted, let's access the function palette *fx* and select IF from the list. You will see the Function Arguments dialog box (Figure 3.12).

There are three things the spreadsheet needs to know:

- **Logical_test** – information the spreadsheet needs to know to make the decision.
- **Value_if_true** – what should happen if the criteria we enter is met.
- **Value_if_false** – what should happen if the criteria we enter is not met.

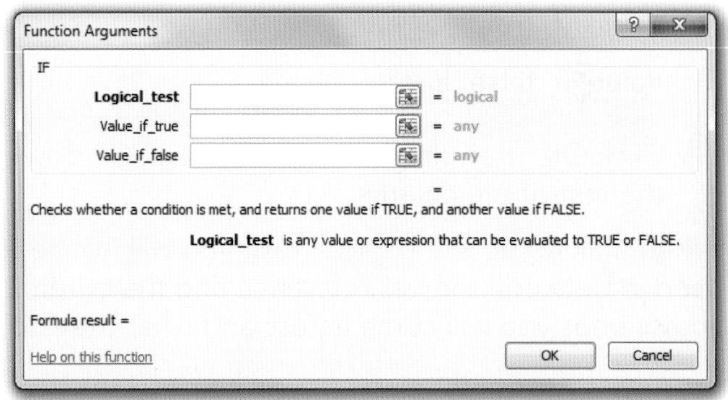

Figure 3.12

So for our example:

Logical_test: B2="Junior". Notice the double quotation marks around the word 'Junior'.

If you are using a word as criteria, you must remember to put double quotation marks around the word or the IF statement will not work.

Value_if_true: 6.75

Value_if_false: 8.75

When the formula is replicated the spreadsheet will look in column B for the word Junior. If it finds this word it will enter £6.75 into column D, but if it can't find the word it will enter £8.75.

You must not type the £ sign into any of the boxes of the IF argument. You should format the cells for currency afterwards. If you do it before, it will cause problems if you want to sort the information later.

Now for an example using a formula.

- Set up a new spreadsheet and add the data shown in Figure 3.13.
- Save the file as **Staff Rewards**.

	A	B	C
1	**Employee**	**Number of years' service**	**Voucher value**
2	Adam	5	
3	Anne	13	
4	Clare	22	
5	Emma	8	
6	Jack	2	
7	Mark	10	

Figure 3.13

To celebrate the organisation's fiftieth birthday, employees are to receive gift vouchers. If the employee has worked for the organisation for ten years or more they will receive a £10 voucher for every year's service. All other employees will get a £5 voucher for every year's service.

We have all the information we need to set up the spreadsheet.

- Click in cell C2, then access the Function Arguments dialog box, as in the example on the previous page, and complete the boxes with the following information.

  Logical_test: B2>=10

  Value_if_true: B2*10

  Value_if_false: B2*5

- Click OK, then drag the corner of cell C2 down to complete the rest of the column.

Symbol	What it means
>	greater than
<	less than
=	equal to
>=	greater than and equal to
<=	less than and equal to

Symbols used in logical tests

When making up the Logical_test, you will notice that symbols are used in between the cell reference and the criteria. The table above shows ones you will come across and what they do.

Named cells (National 5 only)

We know that cells are given a reference and that helps us find our way around the spreadsheet. It is possible for us to give cells a name, to help identify important pieces of information that we might use regularly within a spreadsheet.

We are going to create a summary worksheet to show the total wages that have been paid to all staff.

	A	B
1	**TOTAL STAFF WAGES**	
2	**Name**	**Total Wage**
3	Adam	
4	Anne	
5	Clare	
6	Emma	
7	Jack	
8	Mark	

Figure 3.14

- Using the **Staff Wages** file, create a new worksheet in the workbook and type in the information and use the layout shown in Figure 3.14. Rename the worksheet SUMMARY.
- Let's return to the worksheet for Adam. We are going to give the cell with the total in it a name.

Adam Total | fx =SUM(D8:D8)

	A	B	C	D
1	Week beginning	Number of hours	Rate per hour	Total
2	05/08/2013	10	£6.75	£67.50
3	12/08/2013	12	£6.75	£81.00
4	19/08/2013	14	£6.75	£94.50
5	26/08/2013	12	£6.75	£81.00
6	02/09/2013	12	£6.75	£81.00
7	09/09/2013	14	£6.75	£94.50
8	16/09/2013	25	£6.75	£168.75
9	**TOTAL**			**£168.75**

- Click in cell D9.
- Select Name Manager from the Formulas ribbon.
- Click New and in the Name box key in AdamTotal and click OK. (**Note:** No spaces between the words.)

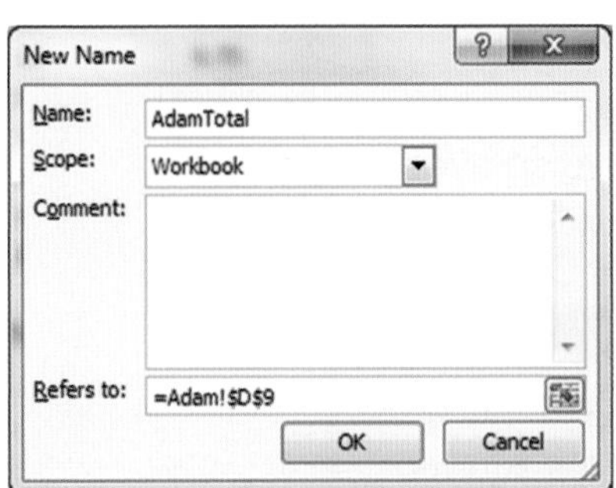

- Now go to the Summary sheet you created, click in cell B9 and key in: =AdamTotal and then click Enter.

You will notice that the value that is in the worksheet for Adam is now displayed in this cell. We have created a link between these two cells.

This is really useful because if the total changes, the value that we see in the summary sheet will automatically update. This saves the time it takes to go and update information in different places, and also means mistakes are less likely because the spreadsheet will not forget to make the change for us.

Named cells* can also be used in formulae. Let's make some changes to Adam's worksheet to see how this works.

- Delete the column Rate per hour (right-click on the column and click Delete).
- Delete all the entries in the Total column (column C).
- In cell A12 key in: Rate per hour.
- In cell B12 key in: £6.75. Name this cell Rate1.
- In cell C2 enter the formula =B2*Rate1 (you can either key in the cell name or click on B12).
- Click Enter and fill down for the remaining rows.
- See Figure 3.15 for how the worksheet should now look.

	A	B	C
1	Week beginning	Number of hours	Total
2	05/08/2013	10	=B2*Rate1
3	12/08/2013	12	
4	19/08/2013	14	
5	26/08/2013	12	
6	02/09/2013	12	
7	09/09/2013	14	
8	16/09/2013	25	
9	**TOTAL**		**£0.00**
10			
11			
12	**Rate per hour**	£6.75	

Figure 3.15

Why have we done this?

First of all, if the rate per hour changes, it only needs to be changed in cell B12 and then totals will update automatically to include this change.

Remember what happens when we fill down? The row and columns in the formula will change; in our example, when we fill down B2 will become B3, then B4, and so on. We want this to happen, as we want the formula to use the hours for the next row in the sheet.

*Note: Using Name Manager allows the user to see all named cells within a workbook and, of course, allows the user to Edit (Rename) or delete (Rename with Cell Reference).

If we hadn't named cell B12 then when we filled down this would also change to B13, B14, and so on. As £6.75 is always in B12, we have to name it to make sure it does not move when used in a formula.

There is another way of making a cell remain in the same place within a formula if you have not named the cell. This is done by pressing the F4 key after you have clicked the cell you want to keep fixed. This makes the cell reference in the formula **absolute**. We call this **relative** or **absolute cell referencing**.

In the example above we would enter our formula as =B2*B12 and after clicking B12 you would press F4 and then click Enter. The formula would be displayed as: =B2*B12. The $ signs mean this cell will not change when you fill down.

Naming cells or using the F4 key are two different ways of doing the same thing; you should use the method that you are most comfortable with.

Changing a named cell

Sometimes you might need to change a named cell. You might have made a mistake and named the wrong cell, decided you want to change the name or no longer need the cell to be named.

Using the Formulas ribbon, click Name Manager. You will be shown a dialog box with all the named cells within the workbook. Click the one you need to change or get rid of and click Delete. Then click Close.

If you need to, you can then go back and name the cell again.

Some things to keep in mind when using named cells:

- Named cells cannot have any spaces. If you include a space when you are naming a cell, the name will not be applied to the cell. If you really want to separate out words, use an underscore.
- Named cells can only be used once in a sheet within the workbook; this means you cannot have two names that are the same within the same file.
- If you need to make a change to a named cell, it is always best to delete it and start again, rather than try and edit it.

Sorting

Often we need to arrange the data in a spreadsheet in a particular order to make it easier to work with. There are lots of different ways of sorting the information, as can be seen in Table 3.2.

Sort	Ascending	Descending
Alphabetically	A–Z	Z–A
Numerically	Smallest to largest	Largest to smallest
Chronologically	Oldest to newest	Newest to oldest

Table 3.2

Let's look at some examples to make these different types of sorts clearer.

Sort	Ascending	Descending
Alphabetically	Adam Anne Clare Emma Jack Mark	Mark Jack Emma Clare Anne Adam
Numerically	£10.20 £11.50 £52.40 £52.80 £86.90 £95.00	£95.00 £86.90 £52.80 £52.40 £11.50 £10.20
Chronologically	08/02/2012 05/06/2012 10/07/2013 11/08/2013 01/01/2014	01/01/2014 11/08/2013 10/07/2013 05/06/2012 08/02/2012

Once we know how we want the data sorted we can instruct the spreadsheet to complete the sort.

It has been decided that the **Staff Wages** spreadsheet is to be sorted in descending order of number of hours worked each week; in other words, we want to see the most number of hours first and the least number of hours last.

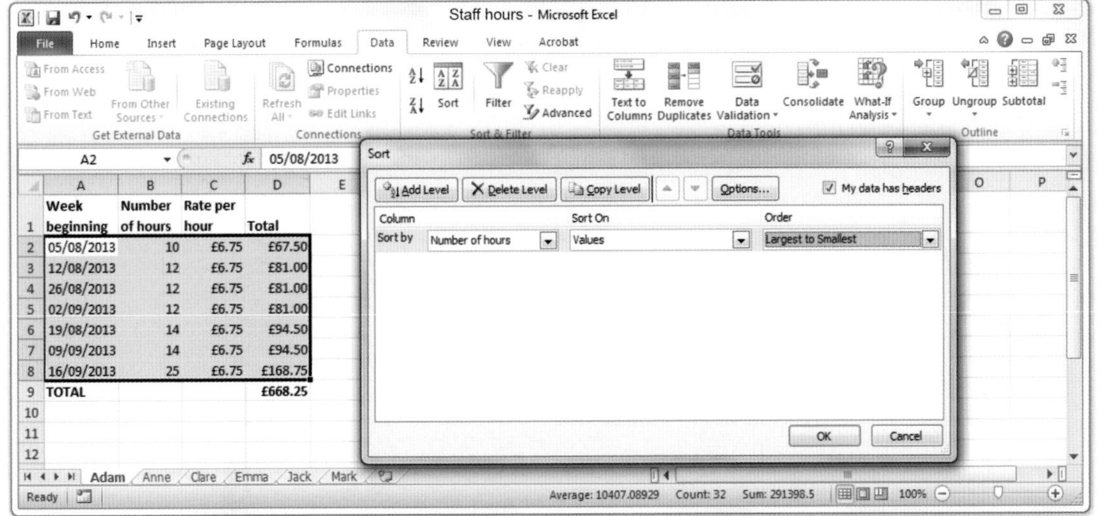

- First, select the data that you want to sort. **Think about this!** The headings and data directly underneath will be used in our sort – we do not want to include the totals, which need to stay at the end – so we will highlight cells **A1:D8**.
- Then from the Data ribbon select Sort.
- In the Sort dialog box we will enter the details of the sort. We want to sort by number of hours and we want it to be in descending order, so we will select Largest to Smallest.

The results we are looking for are shown in Table 3.3.

Week beginning	Number of hours	Rate per hour	Total
16/09/2013	25	£6.75	£168.75
19/08/2013	14	£6.75	£94.50
09/09/2013	14	£6.75	£94.50
12/08/2013	12	£6.75	£81.00
26/08/2013	12	£6.75	£81.00
02/09/2013	12	£6.75	£81.00
05/08/2013	10	£6.75	£67.50
TOTAL			**£668.25**

Table 3.3

We can also sort more than one column. This will group information together when data is similar. Let's look at some examples to see this in action.

In Table 3.4 we have a list of staff and the departments they work in. It would be useful to have all the departments in alphabetical order and then all the staff names in order too.

- Set up a new spreadsheet and add the data shown in Table 3.4.
- Save the file as **Staff Departments**.

Name	Department
Adam	Sales
Anne	Admin
Clare	Finance
Emma	Admin
Jack	Sales
Mark	Finance

Table 3.4

Name	Department
Anne	Admin
Emma	Admin
Clare	Finance
Mark	Finance
Adam	Sales
Jack	Sales

Table 3.5

In table 3.5, you can see that the departments have been sorted first, and then staff are sorted into order next. The steps to take to sort two columns are very similar to how we sorted in the last example.

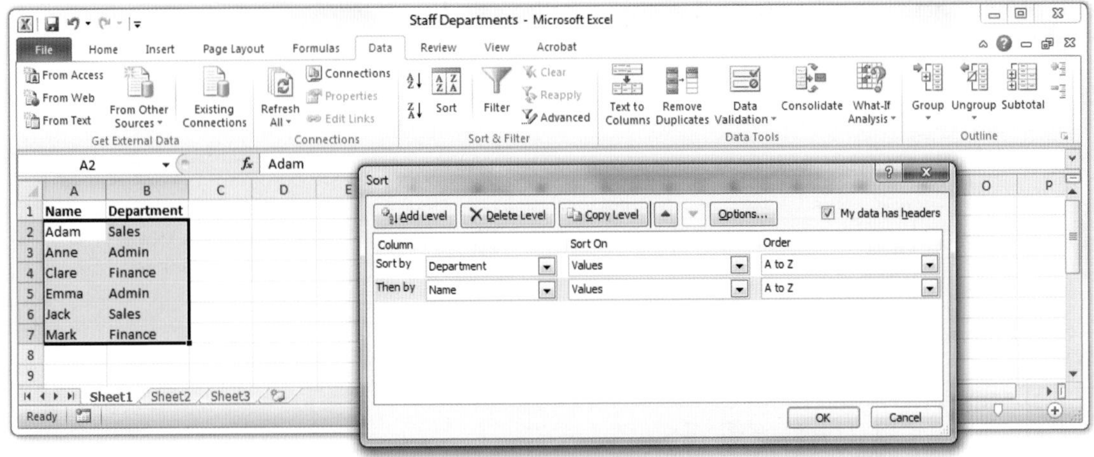

- Highlight the data to be sorted (cells A2:B7).
- Click Sort from the Data ribbon.
- Sort by Department, A–Z.
- Then we have to add another criteria, by clicking Add Level.
- Then sort by Name, A–Z, in the new level.

Charts

Spreadsheets can take the data in a spreadsheet and create charts; this makes analysing the information much easier, and is useful for presenting the information at meetings.

Chart types

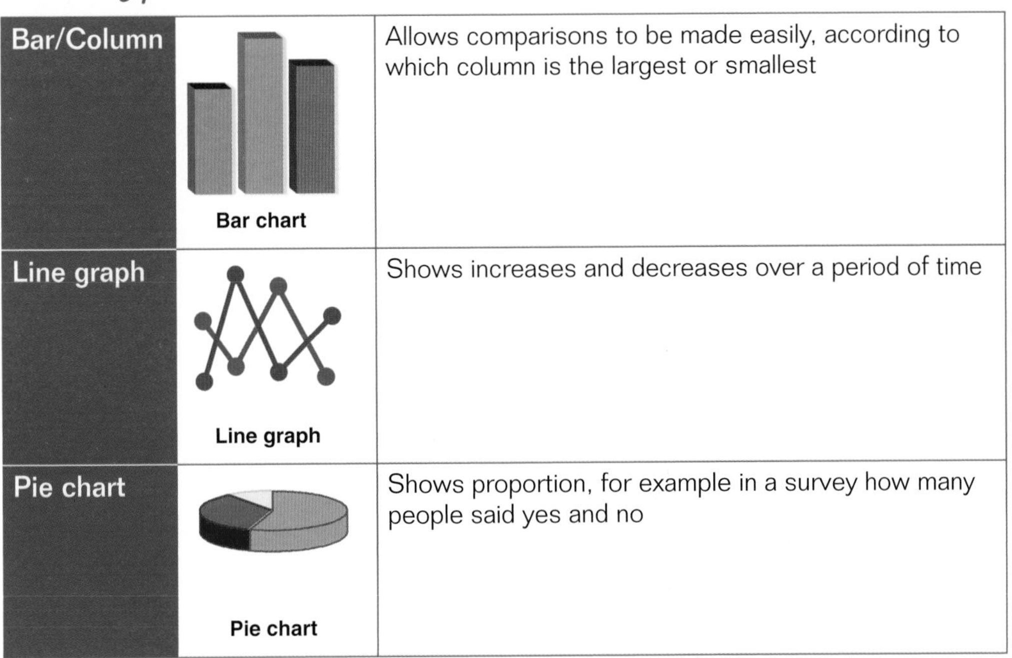

Bar/Column	**Bar chart**	Allows comparisons to be made easily, according to which column is the largest or smallest
Line graph	**Line graph**	Shows increases and decreases over a period of time
Pie chart	**Pie chart**	Shows proportion, for example in a survey how many people said yes and no

So how do we create a chart?

- Set up a new spreadsheet and add the data shown in Figure 3.16, cells A1:B7.
- Save the file as **Staff Hours**.

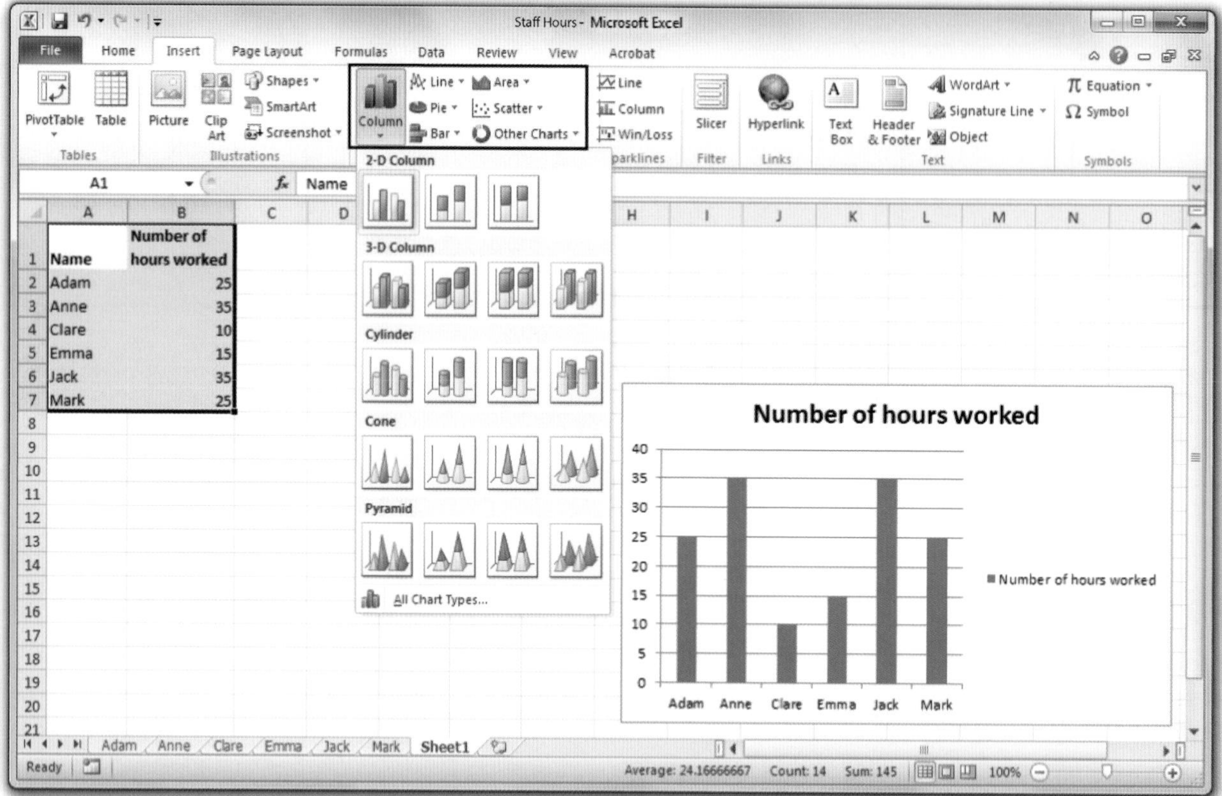

Figure 3.16

- First, highlight the data that is to be included in the chart.
- From the Insert ribbon, select the chart type you want to create, for example column, line or pie. In this example we are creating a column chart. There are lots of versions of this chart type, but it is often best to select the first chart in the menu.
- Your chart will appear on the worksheet.

It is likely there is work still to be done on the chart. You might need to:

- move the chart to a sheet of its own
- edit or add a title
- add or remove a legend, data labels or X/Y-axis titles.

Moving the chart

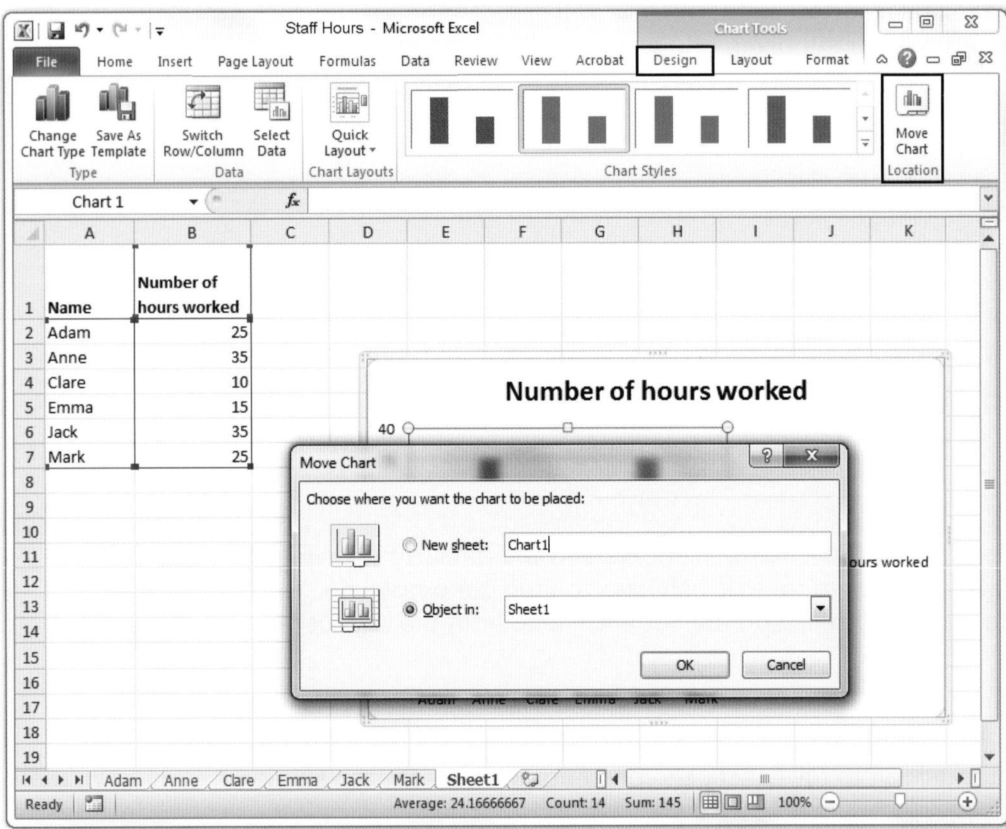

- Make sure you have selected the chart (click on it). This will bring up some extra ribbons to work with.
- From the Design ribbon, click Move Chart.
- Select New Sheet option from the Move Chart dialog box that is displayed, and click OK.
- The chart will now appear on its own, in full screen (Figure 3.17).

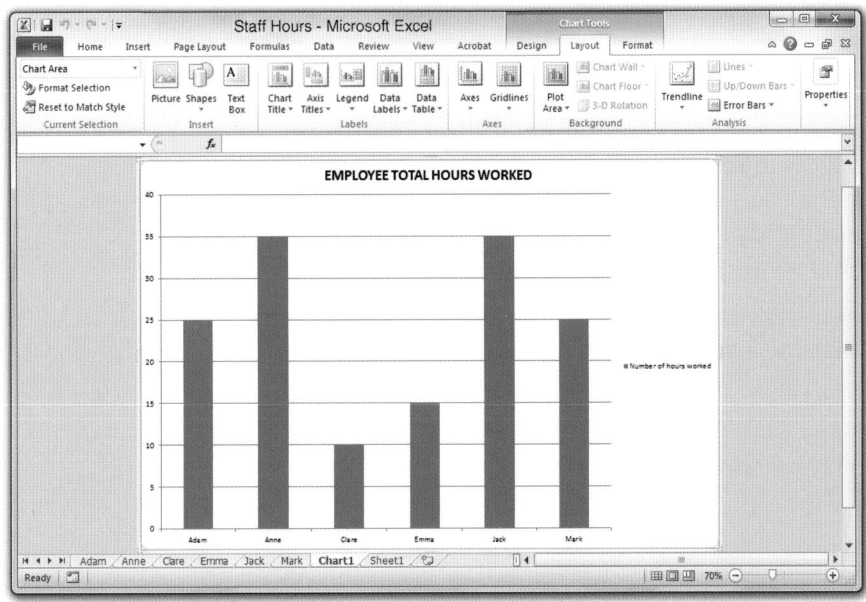

Figure 3.17

Adding/changing the title

Often a chart title will be inserted automatically. You can change this by clicking into the text box and editing the given title to the one you want.

If a title has not been inserted, then a text box can be added by clicking Chart title from the Layout ribbon.

Adding X/Y-axis titles

If your main title clearly explains the content of your chart, then X (horizontal) and Y (vertical) axis titles are not needed. In Figure 3.17 on the previous page, names are on the X-axis and numbers along the Y-axis, and the title explains that the names are employees and the numbers are hours worked. Labels are not needed.

If you want to add the labels, you can insert text boxes by selecting Axis Titles from the Layout ribbon.

Legend

This should only be displayed if it helps to understand the data. Again in Figure 3.17, the legend isn't needed, as there is only one column per employee. You can add and remove a legend by selecting the Legend menu from the Layout ribbon.

Data labels

These give more information to help interpret the chart. They are mostly used in a pie chart, where it is difficult to tell exactly the percentage value of each section.

Sometimes the information we want to include in a chart is not always next to each other (adjacent). Other columns or rows that we don't want to include in the chart might be in the way. The easiest way to overcome this problem is to hide the columns or rows you do not want and then they can be brought back when the chart is created. *See page 32.*

Printing

In the modern office and with the increasing use of mobile devices such as smartphones and tablets that allow information to be accessed electronically from any location, printed materials are not needed as often. There are, however, occasions when a paper copy is requested, and there are steps that have to be taken when printing a spreadsheet to make sure it is useful.

Here is a list of the possible requests work colleagues may make when printing a spreadsheet; often they will ask for a combination of these for one printout:

- landscape or portrait
- with or without gridlines
- with or without row and column headings
- values or formulae view
- all on one page
- extracts (only certain parts of the spreadsheet).

Where there are no specific requests made for printing other than to print, then both the following views should be printed and rules followed:

- formulae view: landscape, gridlines and row and column headings
- values view: landscape and gridlines.

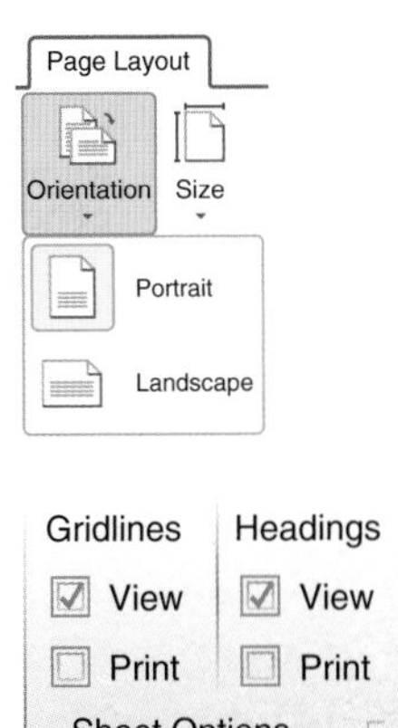

Portrait/landscape orientation

Spreadsheets are automatically set to be in portrait orientation. You can check and change, if necessary, the orientation of the printout through the Page Layout ribbon.

Gridlines and row/column headings

Through the Page Layout ribbon, gridlines and row/column headings can be added or removed when printed by ticking the relevant boxes.

Printing on one page

The spreadsheet can be scaled so it will all fit on one page. This setting is found in the print menu (File > Print). Then from the dropdown menu, which will state 'No Scaling', select 'Fit Sheet on One Page', which you can see below:

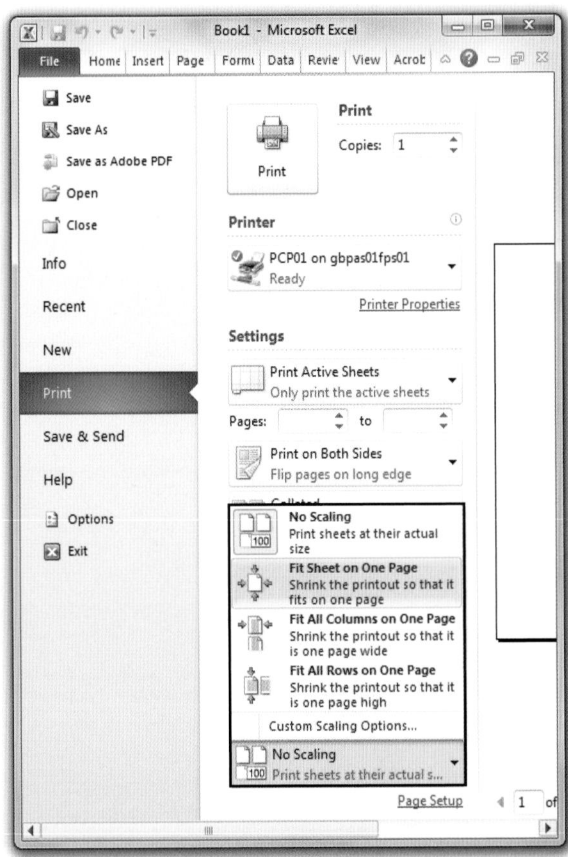

Printing value and formulae view

Value view

	A	B	C	D
1	**Week beginning**	**Number of hours**	**Rate per hour**	**Total**
2	05/08/2013	10	£6.75	£67.50
3	12/08/2013	12	£6.75	£81.00
4	19/08/2013	14	£6.75	£94.50
5	26/08/2013	12	£6.75	£81.00
6	02/09/2013	12	£6.75	£81.00
7	09/09/2013	14	£6.75	£94.50
8	16/09/2013	25	£6.75	£168.75
9	**TOTAL**			**£668.25**

Formulae view

To show formulae, select Show Formulas from the Formulas ribbon OR press the control key and accent key on your keyboard at the same time.

	A	B	C	D
1	**Week beginning**	**Number of hours**	**Rate per hour**	**Total**
2	41491	10	6.75	=B2*C2
3	41498	12	6.75	=B3*C3
4	41505	14	6.75	=B4*C4
5	41512	12	6.75	=B5*C5
6	41519	12	6.75	=B6*C6
7	41526	14	6.75	=B7*C7
8	41533	25	6.75	=B8*C8
9	**TOTAL**			**=SUM(D2:D8)**

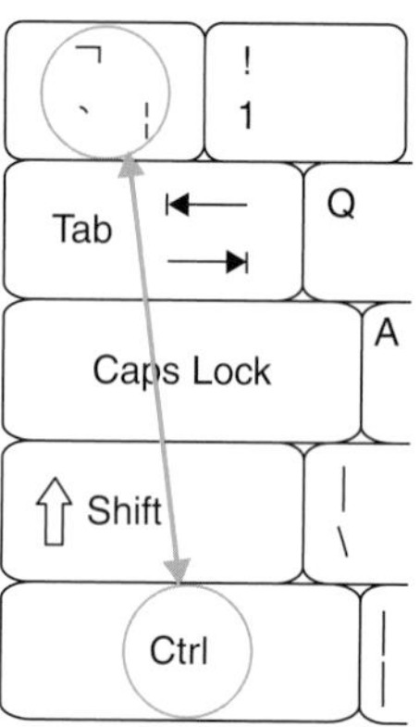

Before printing, make sure to double-check all text is visible. Sometimes when changing to formulae view, the column width is not increased enough to see the entire formulae and you will need to change this.

National 4 & 5 task

Complete the following Skills Scan to check your learning. Use the file **Chapter 3 Spreadsheets Skills Scan**. Tick the box that applies to each task.

I can	**easily**	**not sure**	**have difficulty**
Create and edit spreadsheets			
Insert and edit data			
Insert/delete columns/rows			
Apply cell borders and shading			
Cell alignment			
Format cells for			
Currency			
Date			
Percentages			
Use comments			
Insert basic formula			
Add			
Subract			
Multiply			
Divide			
Use basic functions			
Sum			
Average			
Minimum			
Maximum			
CountA			
CountBLANK			
Sort data			
Print value view – one page			
Print formulae view – one page			

Print with/without gridlines			
Print with row/column headings			
Charts			
Create a simple chart			
Label charts			
Print charts			
National 5 only: Format Cells for			
Condional formatting			
National 5 only: Use advanced functions			
CountIF			
IF			
Linked worksheets			
Named cells			
Absolute/relative cell references			
National 5 only: Charts			
Create a chart from non-adjacent data			

IT Solutions for Administrators

Chapter 4
Use of database applications to support admin tasks

By the end of this chapter you will:

- ✓ understand the purpose and uses of databases within organisations
- ✓ develop skills in creating and editing databases
- ✓ develop skills in using the functions of databases to manage and manipulate information.

Information can be stored in paper format (for example telephone directories, timetables for train journeys, catalogues for toys, electronic equipment and jewellery) *or* electronic format (for example smartphone contacts list, apps for train journeys).

P

Parsons, India, 64 James Road	01796 352 945
Parsons, Michelle, 64 James Road	01796 352 945
Parsons, Mike, 64 James Road	01796 352 945
Parsons, Seb, 64 James Road	01796 352 945
Patel, Dev, 16 South Street	01796 352 945
Patel, Raj, 16 South Street	01796 352 945
Patel, Vokram, 16 South Street	01796 352 945

R

Randall, Alan, 26 North Road	01796 362 131
Randall, Ellan, 26 North Road	01796 362 131
Reed, Claire, 26 North Road	01796 362 131
Reed, Gavin, 26 North Road	01796 362 131
Reed, Peter, 49 Passage Road	01796 362 131
Riddle, Terry, 9 Other Road	01796 36
Riddle, Wayne, 9 Other Road	01796 36

ELECTRONICS
GREAT GIFTS......
£69.99
BEST BUY
£209.99
BEST BUY
£79.95
BEST BUY
£37.00
BEST BUY

The information is organised in such a way that it allows you to find the right information at the right time and presented in the right format.

All organisations (from small local businesses to large organisations) collect, process and transmit large amounts of information. It is important that this information is stored so that it too can be found and presented in the right format.

Most organisations use a database to store this information electronically.

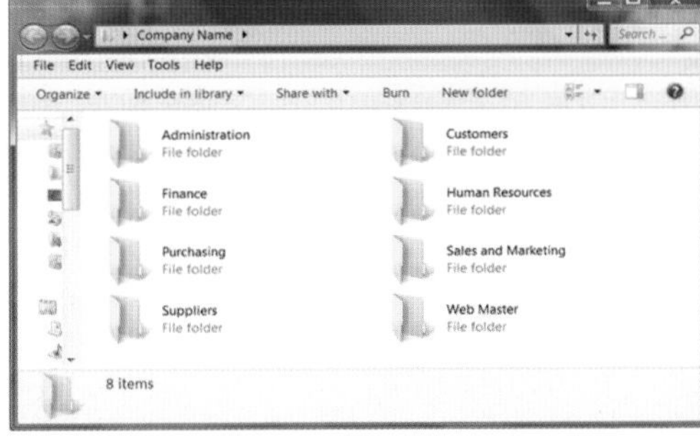

Databases can be used by multiple users at the same time. Having one central copy of a database means all staff have access to the most accurate and up-to-date information. If changes are made, everyone can see the changes immediately.

Database basics

Before you start using a database make sure you understand the terms in Table 4.1.

Database	In the Microsoft Access® software program, this is the main *file* where everything is stored. It is a bit like an electronic *filing cabinet*.
Table	A table is laid out in rows and columns rather like a spreadsheet. It might contain an address list or a price list. In Access® you can store a number of tables within a database file.
Field	A field is like a heading that you store data under. Most tables will contain a number of fields, for example in an address table the fields might include: Surname, First Name, Street, Town, Postcode.
Record	A record is an individual entry, for example in an address table there would be a record for each person, with data in each field.
Cell	This usually refers to a particular field in a particular record, for example the Surname field in the first record of a table.
Form	A form is a way to enter data into a database. It is much better to enter data this way as you only view one record at a time.
Query	This is a feature of the database which allows the user to search and find specific information from a table or from a number of tables within a database (sometimes referred to as Find.) In other words, you tell the computer to select records which contain certain information (criteria) only.
Report	A report is a way to display data in an interesting and professional way. Access® has a number of ready-made design formats to choose from or you can design your own. You can create a report from a table, or a query. You can select the fields you want displayed in your report and you can also sort the data in a number of fields. Reports can also be used to create labels very easily.

Table 4.1

Data is stored in tables within the database. This is then broken down into similar groups, called **fields**.

Let's look at an example to see how this works in practice. The two notes on the following page contain the personal information of customers. The database has yet to be designed to enter this information. The first task is to decide how to group the information. Although the information is for different people, it contains similar information; think how you might group this information.

Miss Clare West
31 Riverbank Wynd
Glasgow
G4 5LK
0141 021 3661
08/02/1986

Mr Mark Pickering
15 Albion Square
Glasgow
G1 6MN
0141 881 4446
21/08/1984

Here are two possible approaches to grouping this information:

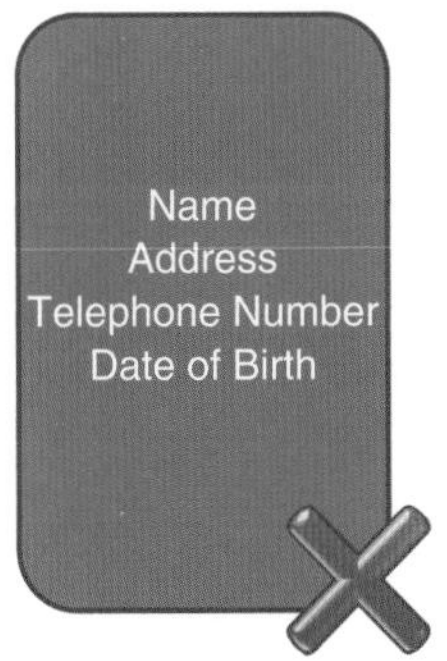

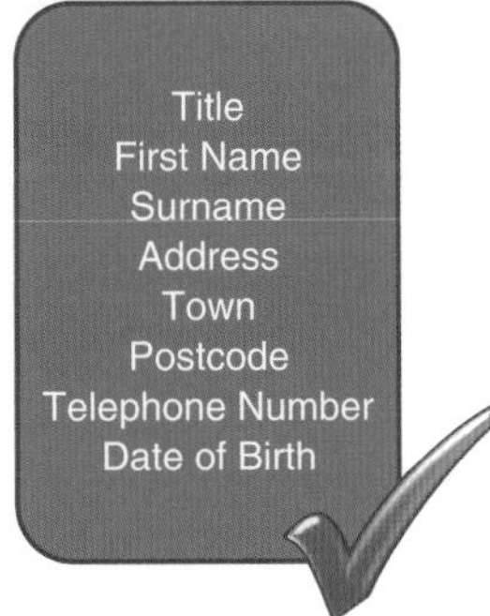

Notice the way that the second list breaks the data down into more groups than the first list. This is the best approach to setting up the database, as separating the information as much as possible makes looking for information later much easier to do.

Why?

Think about it. If you want to look for customers from Glasgow, it will be much easier to locate these customers when the town is separated out from the rest of the address. So, when setting up fields within a record in a database it is always important to make sure you have broken down the data into as many groups as is possible.

Once data is entered into the database it is stored in a table, as shown in Figure 4.1.

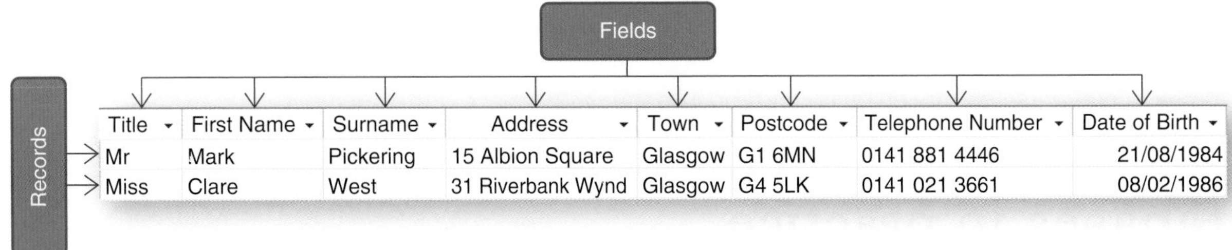

Title	First Name	Surname	Address	Town	Postcode	Telephone Number	Date of Birth
Mr	Mark	Pickering	15 Albion Square	Glasgow	G1 6MN	0141 881 4446	21/08/1984
Miss	Clare	West	31 Riverbank Wynd	Glasgow	G4 5LK	0141 021 3661	08/02/1986

Figure 4.1

Designing a table

This involves deciding on field names and defining the data types and formats for each field. Therefore, before creating the fields in the table, thought has to go into the type of information that is being entered into the database. Each field has to be given a suitable name which reflects the content. Also, to help the database understand how we want to sort or find information, it has to be told the type of information in each field.

There are two types of data contained in the table shown: text and date.

Wait! Why are there only **two** types of data in the table with the customer details? Shouldn't 'number' be a type of data for telephone number?

No, it's not a mistake.

Telephone number has to be set as **text**; if you don't do this then the '0' at the start will always disappear.

There are many other types of data you can select; Table 4.2 shows some of the most common that you will come across.

Data Type	Description	Possible extra format
Text	Text fields can include letters, numbers and symbols, or a combination of these, e.g. Peter *or* PTR-234	Not necessary
Number	Number fields should include only plain, ordinary numbers, such as 1234 – not dates or currency. No text can be stored in a number field. Telephone numbers, which begin with 0, cannot be formatted as numbers but must be left as text.	Not necessary
Date/Time	This is a type of number formatting for including either a date, such as 14/09/14 or 14 September 2014, or a time, such as 10.35pm or 2235 hours.	Short, Medium or Long date am/pm or 24 hours
Currency	Currency fields contain a number formatted as money, such as £20.00 or £20.	Decimal places can be changed
Yes/No	This will display a check box which can be ticked (Yes) or left blank (No).	Can be changed to a text box – Yes/No

Table 4.2

Setting the field data type not only helps the database when you want to search and sort but also prevents information being entered into the wrong place, for example if you try to enter a postcode into the date of birth field, the database will not allow it.

Databases in practice

Let's have a go at working with a database to see what it can do. The **Staff** database has been designed to store information about employees that work at an organisation. It contains two tables – one with personal information about them, called **Staff Details**, and one with information about the branch they work in, called **Branches**. The information in each table is related, to avoid repeating the branch details where each employee works. Open the **Staff** database.

Editing the database table

The table is where all the data we enter is stored. Organisations often decide they need to collect additional information and so new fields have to be added to the database.

It has been decided to add a field, Length of Service, to the staff details table. Here is the information that is to be added:

Clare	10	Sam	3
Mark	4	Anne	14
Amir	17	Karine	1
Laura	1	Adam	8
Paula	3	Eilidh	9
Tom	4	Emma	16
Leanne	13	Campbell	4
Julie	2	Jay	12
Shazia	11	Claire	11
Gavin	10	Kerrie	3
Alistair	15		

When setting up a new field follow these steps:

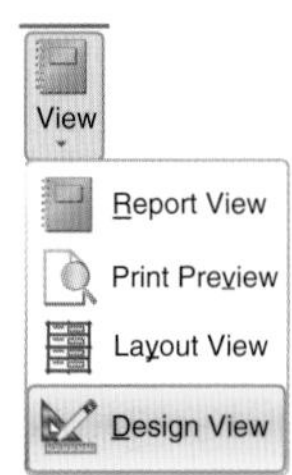

- Change to Design View by clicking [View] at the top right-hand corner of the screen.
- You will be taken to the Design View and see the list of fields that are in the staff details table.

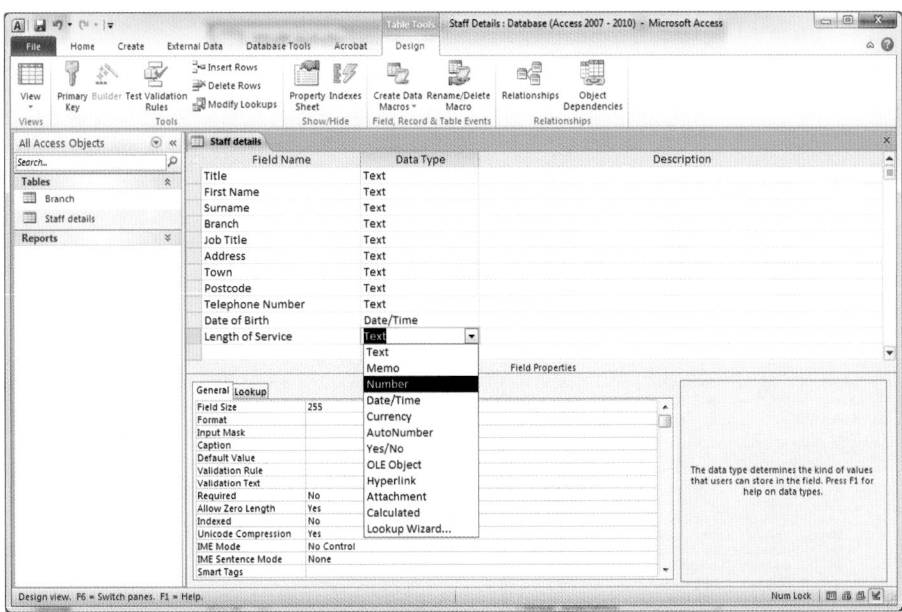

- Click in the row under Date of Birth and key in: Length of Service.
- Select Number from the Data Type menu
- Click [View] at the top left-hand corner of the screen to take you back to the data.

You will see there is now a new field added and the new data can be entered.

You will notice that a database often contains a lot of repetitive information; in the database in this example, Title and Branch are fields that have similar information. To speed up data entry and to reduce keying-in errors, a list can be set up to choose from, rather than keying in the information. This is called a **'Lookup Wizard'**.

Here's how to create a Lookup Wizard:

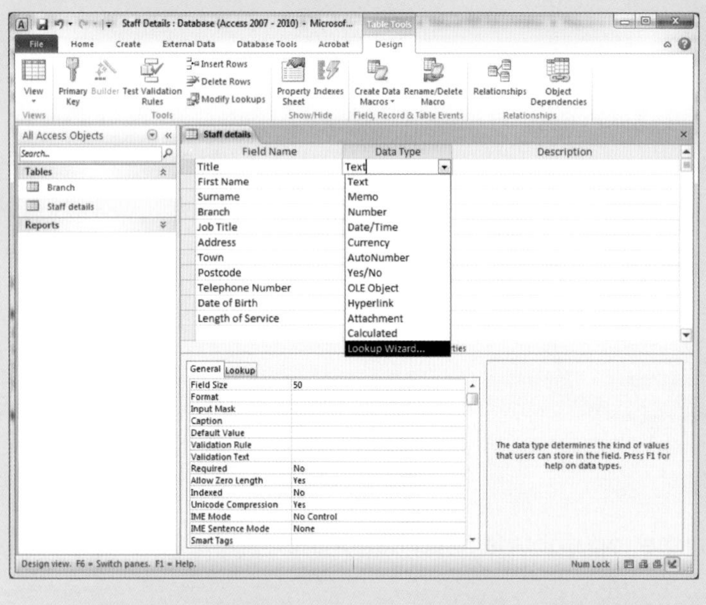

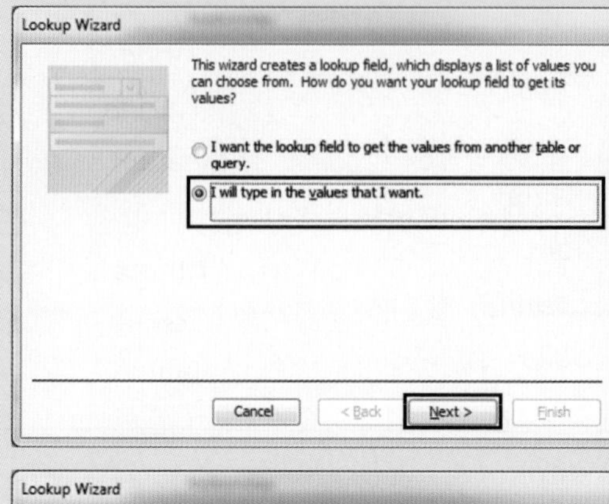

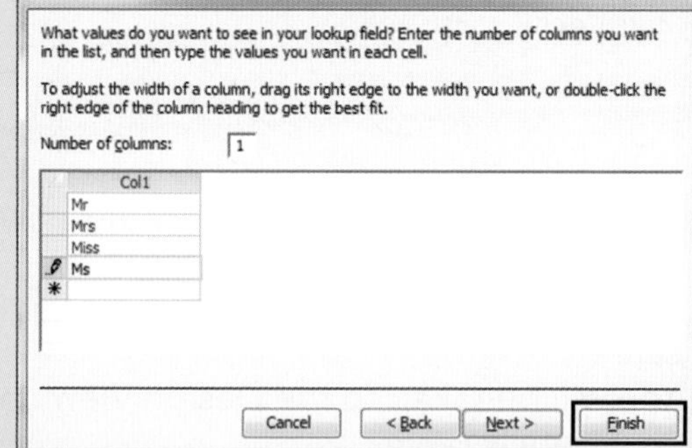

- Select Lookup Wizard from the dropdown menu within the Data type column.
- Select: I will type in the values that I want and click Next.
- Enter the text you would like to include in your list and click Finish.

As well as adding fields, decisions might be made to remove a field completely from the database.

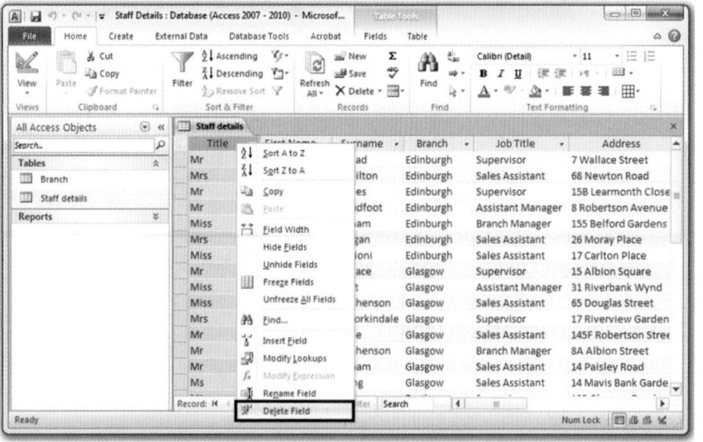

- Right-click on the heading of the field you want to delete.
- From the menu select Delete field.
- You will be asked to confirm you want to delete this field. Click Yes if you are sure. You cannot undo this once you have clicked Yes.

> Don't worry if you find you have missed something out of the list; the database will still let you type in an entry that is not in the list or you can go back into Design View and change the Lookup Wizard to include any new or missing options.

Adding and editing records

New records will often be added, changed or even deleted from the database. This is best completed by using a **form**. A form displays records from the table, one at a time, for viewing and making amendments.

There are a number of reasons for using a form, but the main one is that only one record is shown at a time. This prevents changes being made to the wrong record. In Table View, with so many records on view at once, it is easy to lose your place and change the record above or below. This could have disastrous consequences; imagine if someone else's address was changed by accident and personal information was sent out to the wrong person!

Let's make a form for the Staff details table.

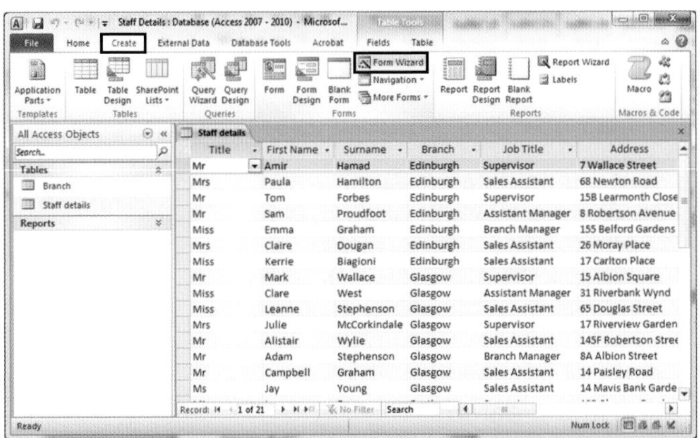

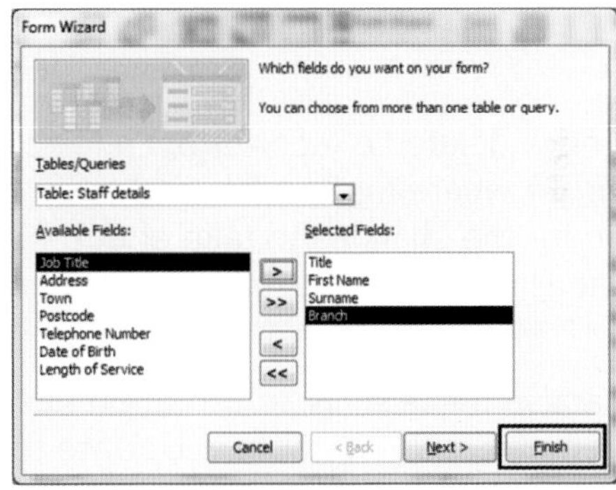

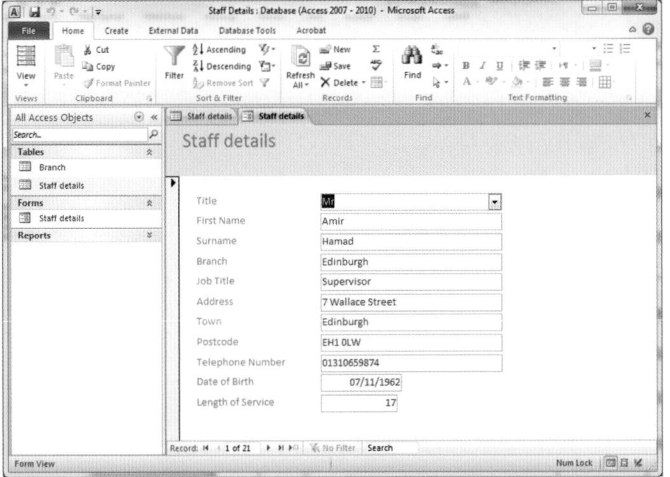

- From the Create ribbon, select Form Wizard.
- You will be then asked to select which fields you want to include in the form. In the box on the left are the fields that are available to include in the form and the box on the right lists the fields we have selected to include in the form.
- We want to include all the fields in this form and so can click >> and then Finish.

> **i**
>
> Sometimes you are asked to include only certain fields in the form. Click on the field you want to include and click >. This will move only one field name over at a time.
>
> If you pick the wrong one you can remove it by selecting the field and clicking <.

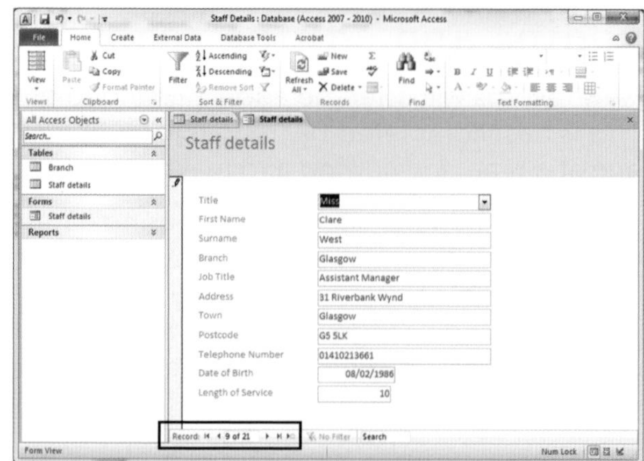

Now we have our form, we can make changes to data within the record simply by deleting the information and typing in the new information or by deleting a record completely:

- Find the record you need to amend or delete by using the arrows at the bottom of the form.
- Make the changes you need, or if you need to delete the record click the long grey bar on the left of the form and it will turn black.
- Press Delete on your keyboard.
- You will be asked to confirm you want to delete the record. Remember you cannot undo actions in a database, so make sure you are deleting the right record before clicking Yes.

If you have deleted a record from a form and go to view the table and see #DELETE# where the record used to be, you must close the table and open it again for the changes to take effect. It's best to make sure the table is not open at all when you are making changes through the form.

Let's practise these skills. Information has been received which requires changes to the records in the database. Update the information in the database.

National 4 & 5 task

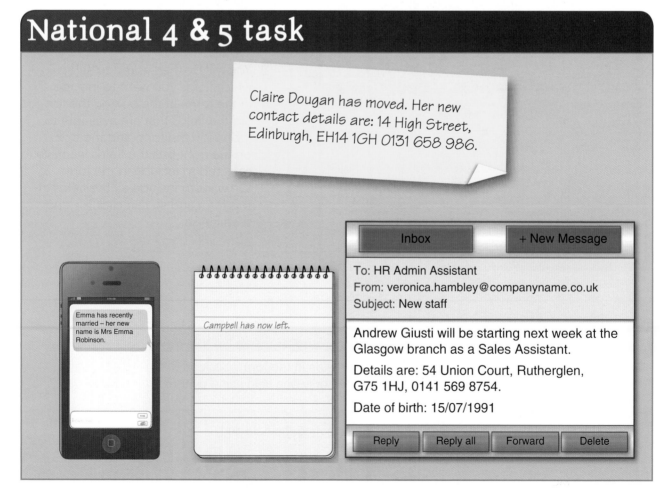

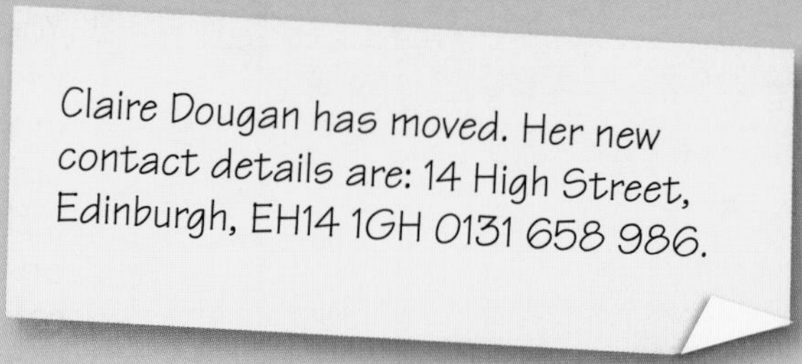

Claire Dougan has moved. Her new contact details are: 14 High Street, Edinburgh, EH14 1GH 0131 658 986.

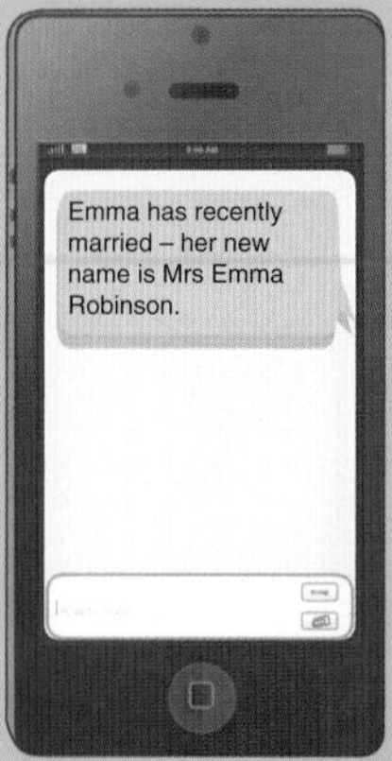

Emma has recently married – her new name is Mrs Emma Robinson.

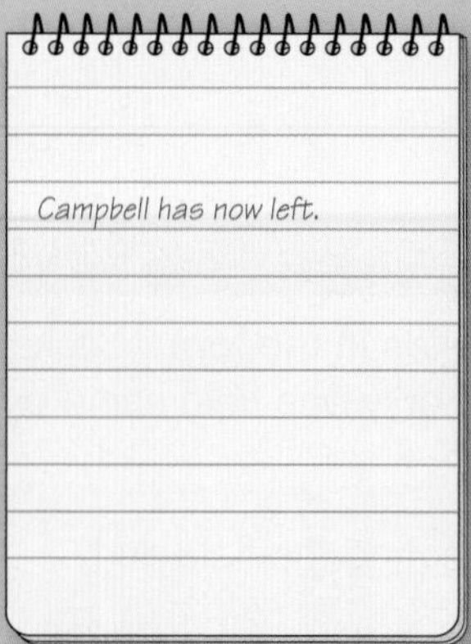

Campbell has now left.

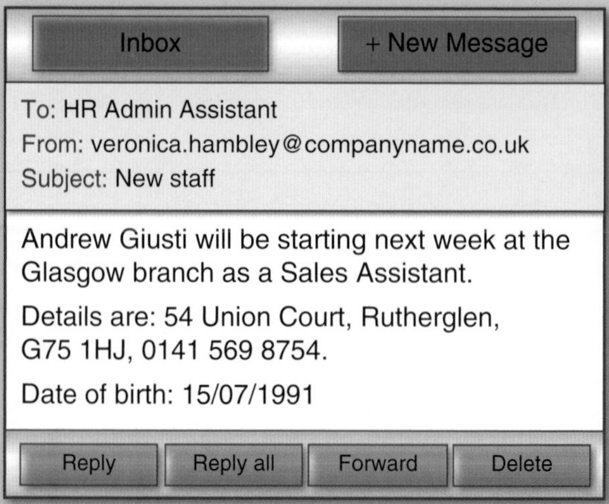

Inbox | + New Message

To: HR Admin Assistant
From: veronica.hambley@companyname.co.uk
Subject: New staff

Andrew Giusti will be starting next week at the Glasgow branch as a Sales Assistant.

Details are: 54 Union Court, Rutherglen, G75 1HJ, 0141 569 8754.

Date of birth: 15/07/1991

Reply | Reply all | Forward | Delete

Searching

As we have seen, the database stores lots of information. We are able to view individual records by making use of a form. Sometimes it is necessary to view certain records and selected fields and in a database we can search for this information (often referred to as a query).

The search must have a criteria, that is, what we are looking for. The criteria can simply be a word or number, for example if we only wanted to see people who lived in Glasgow, our criteria would be Glasgow in the Town field.

It is also possible to look for a range of information when working with numbers, dates or currency. We might want to find staff who were born in or before 1990, so the criteria would be <=31/12/1990.

The table below shows the four different operators that can be used to show ranges.

>	greater than	>=	greater than and equal to
<	less than	<=	less than and equal to

There is also a final type of search that we need to be aware of. This is when looking for two or more entries in a field. A search might need to locate staff from Edinburgh, Glasgow or Perth only. The criteria for this type of search would be entered as Edinburgh or Glasgow or Perth. The word OR must appear between each criteria. This also works when looking for particular numbers.

The database can also accept more than one criteria, so we might want to find staff who live in Glasgow and who were born in or before 1990. There is no limit to the number of criteria that can be entered.

Now we'll have a look at how to search a database.

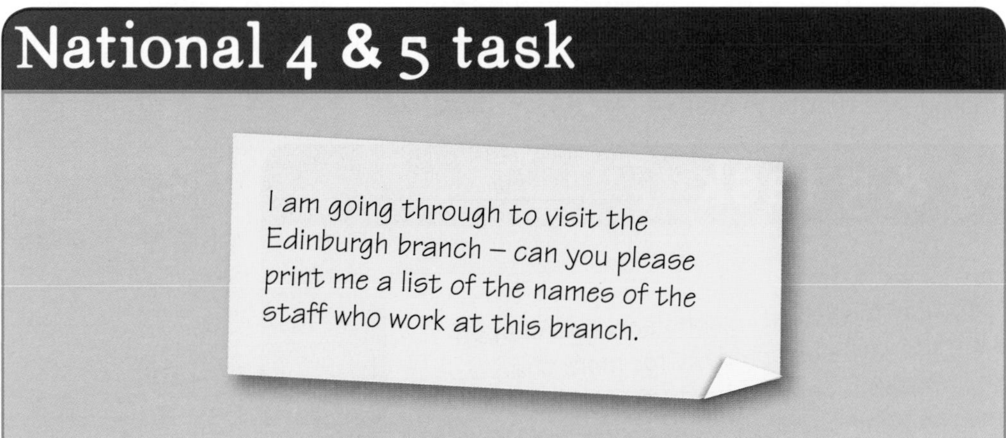

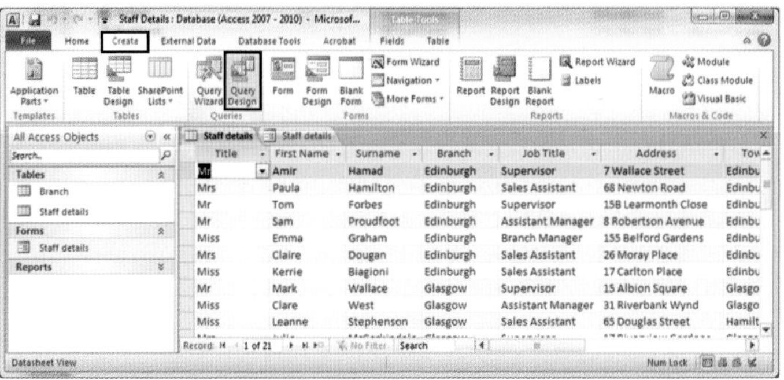

From the Create ribbon, click Query Design.

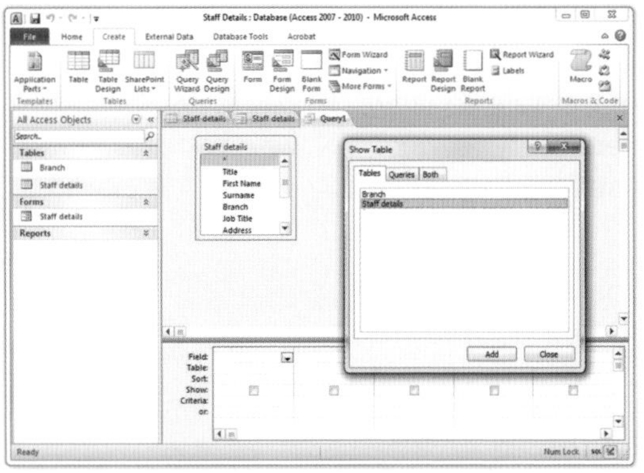

- You will then be asked to select tables to include in the query design. As we are only using the staff details table, double-click this option from the list and click Close.

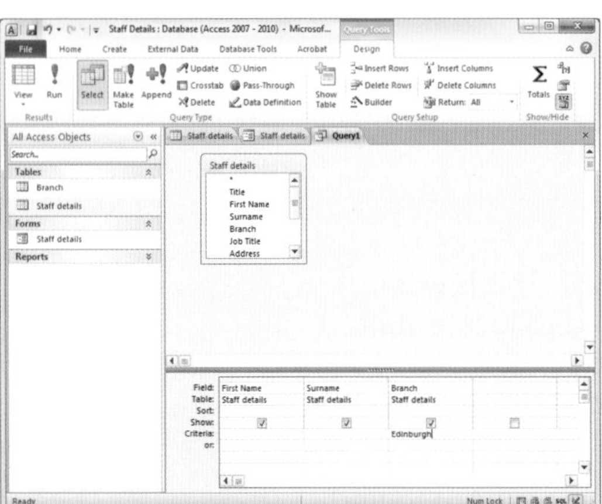

- You will then see a list of fields from the staff details table shown and a grid. This is where we will set up the query.
- We want to produce a list of names of staff from the Edinburgh branch, so let's select those fields to be part of the query.
- Double-click on First Name, Surname and Branch. They will appear in the grid below.
- We only want to see staff from the Edinburgh branch, so in the grid, underneath Branch, key in Edinburgh as the criteria.
- Then click ! Run from the ribbon.

A table will be shown with only the names of staff from the Edinburgh branch. We know that all these staff are from the Edinburgh branch, so do we really need to see Edinburgh repeated all the time? Let's go and make a change to the query. Click View to go back to the Query Design view. Remove the tick from the grid in the column where Branch is displayed. This means that the criteria will stay but when we view the results of the query only the names of the staff will be shown. Close the query, and don't forget to save it. Call the query Edinburgh Staff.

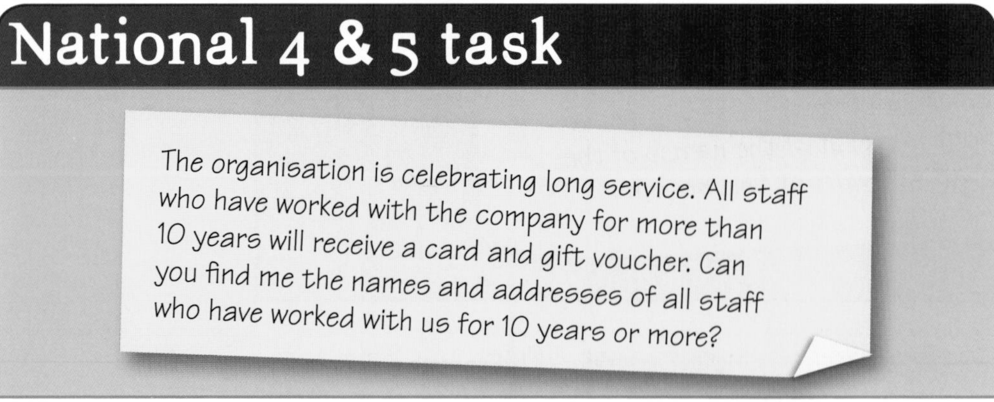

National 4 & 5 task
The organisation is celebrating long service. All staff who have worked with the company for more than 10 years will receive a card and gift voucher. Can you find me the names and addresses of all staff who have worked with us for 10 years or more?

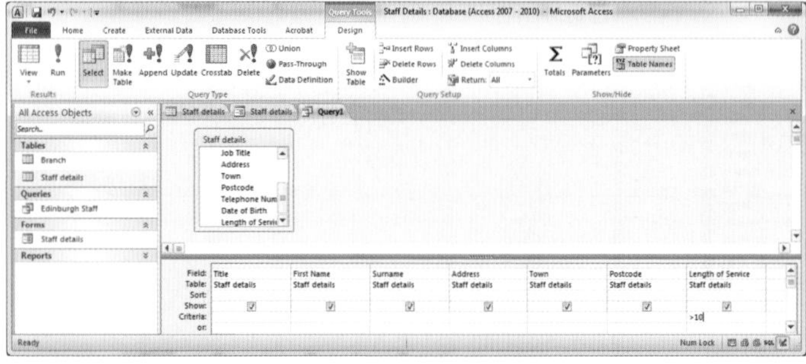

It is also possible to have more than one criteria in a search and to search from more than one table (in a relational database).

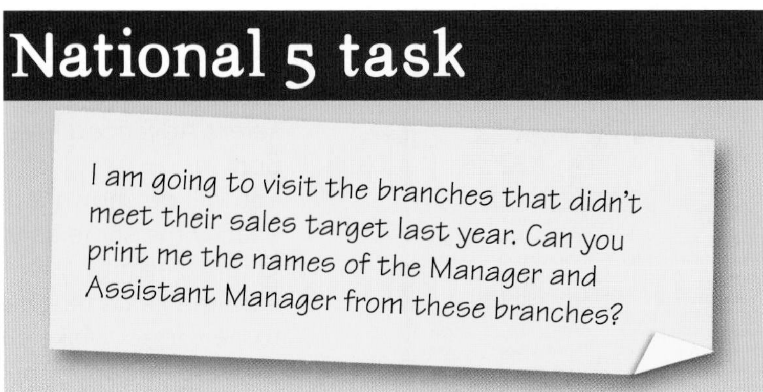

National 5 task
I am going to visit the branches that didn't meet their sales target last year. Can you print me the names of the Manager and Assistant Manager from these branches?

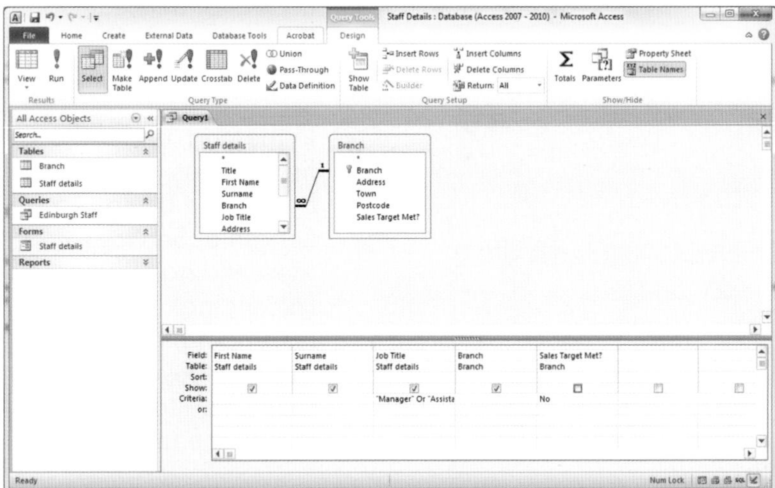

- From the Create ribbon, click Query Design.
- Add Staff Details and Branches from the list of tables and click Close.
- From the list of fields, double click on First Name, Surname and Job Title from the Staff Details list and Branch and Sales Target Met? from the Branches list. They will appear in the grid below.
- We only want to see the names of the Managers and Assistant Managers from the branches that have not met their sales targets, so key in Manager or Assistant Manager as the criteria for job title and No as the criteria for sales target met?
- Uncheck the tick box under Sales Target met? Then click ! (Run) from the ribbon.

Sorting

Requests are often received to sort the data in a table or query, to make it easier to view. There are two ways of sorting: on one field or on multiple fields.

The staff table might need to be sorted in order of date of birth, showing the youngest person first.

- Click the arrow next to the Date of Birth field heading.
- Click: Sort Newest to Oldest.

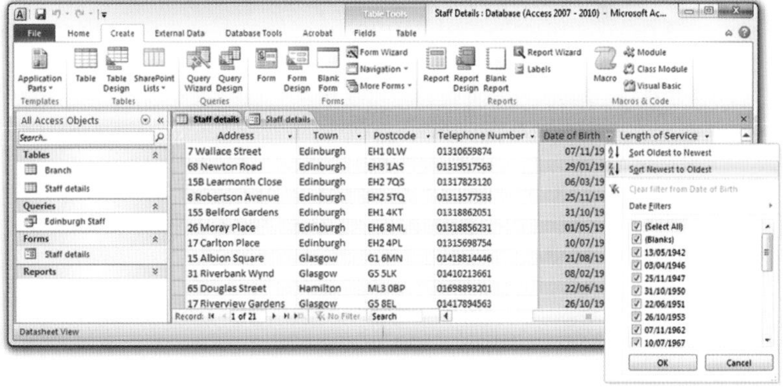

When sorting on more than one field, there are a few more steps that have to be taken. Let's sort the table by showing employees with the longest service first and then alphabetically by name.

- From the Home ribbon click Advanced and select Advanced Filter/Sort.
- You will be shown a grid, exactly the same as the Query Design view.
- Add the fields that need to be sorted. Make sure they are added in the order they are requested: Length of Service, Surname, then First Name.

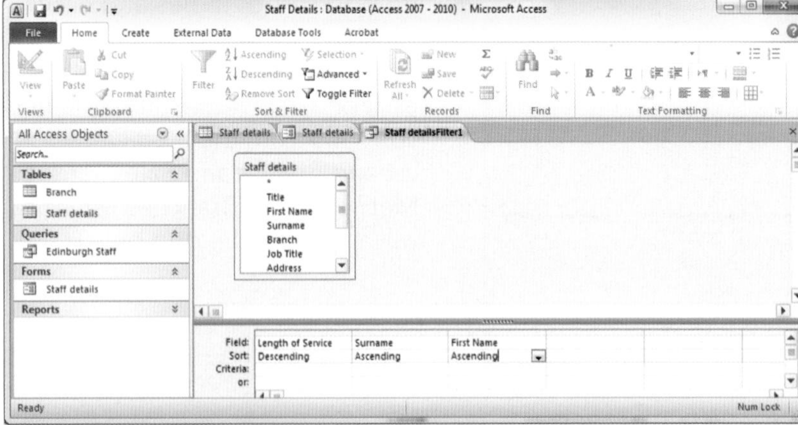

- In the grid, under the field names, select how they are to be sorted: Length of Service (descending), Surname (ascending), First Name (ascending).
- Click Toggle Filter from the ribbon to apply the sort to the table.

Database tables and queries do not remember the sorts you applied to them once you have closed the file down. If you come back to the database at a later date, you should not assume the sort you applied is still there. You will have to do it again.

Reports

The report function in a database is where we are able to prepare information, from tables or queries, to be printed or displayed in another document.

Reports have a number of formatting features that are not available in the table or query view, such as:

- changing font, size and format
- highlighting headings
- inserting **graphics** (the company logo, for example)
- adding information into the header and footer
- wrapping text.

These features improve the presentation of the information; ideal for when presenting to customers or colleagues.

	First Name	Surname	Branch	Job Title
1	Kerrie	Biagioni	Edinburgh	Sales Assistant
2	Claire	Dougan	Edinburgh	Sales Assistant
3	Tom	Forbes	Edinburgh	Supervisor
4	Emma	Graham	Edinburgh	Branch Manager
5	Amir	Hamad	Edinburgh	Supervisor
6	Paula	Hamilton	Edinburgh	Sales Assistant
7	Sam	Proudfoot	Edinburgh	Assistant Manager

Figure 4.2 Query table

Edinburgh Staff

Title	First Name	Surname	Branch	Job Title
Mr	Amir	Hamad	Edinburgh	Supervisor
Mrs	Paula	Hamilton	Edinburgh	Sales Assistant
Mr	Tom	Forbes	Edinburgh	Supervisor
Mr	Sam	Proudfoot	Edinburgh	Assistant Manager
Miss	Emma	Graham	Edinburgh	Branch Manager
Mrs	Claire	Dougan	Edinburgh	Sales Assistant
Miss	Kerrie	Biagioni	Edinburgh	Sales Assistant

Figure 4.3 Report

Let's look at the steps needed to be taken to create a report of the query created earlier, showing only the names of Edinburgh staff.

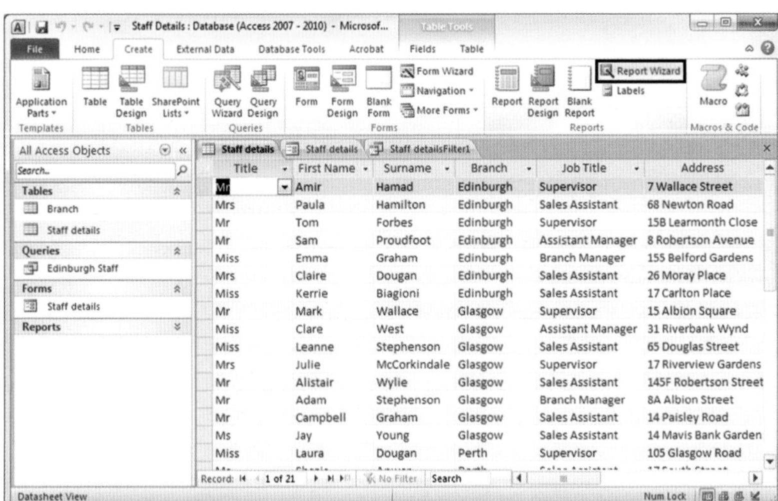

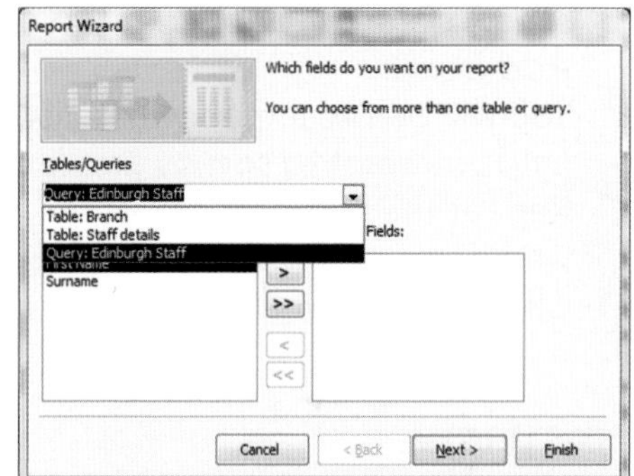

- From the Create ribbon, click Report Wizard.
- From the dropdown menu, select the table or query you want to make a report from. This time we want to use Query Edinburgh Staff.
- We want to include all Fields so can click >>. Remember if you only want certain fields, move them across using >. Click Next.
- We will not be adding any grouping levels, so just click Next again.
- We won't be sorting the report just yet, so just click Next again.
- We want to display the report in landscape, so can change that here. It is likely that portrait view will never be wide enough for any report, unless you are only including two or three fields, so it's always best to go with landscape to give you more space. Click Next.
- A report **must always** include a heading. The heading should explain what the information in the report shows. In this example the report shows staff in the Edinburgh branch – so let's call it Edinburgh Staff and click Finish.

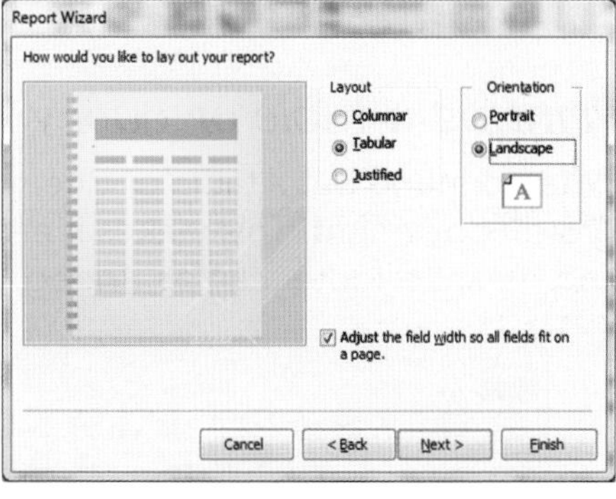

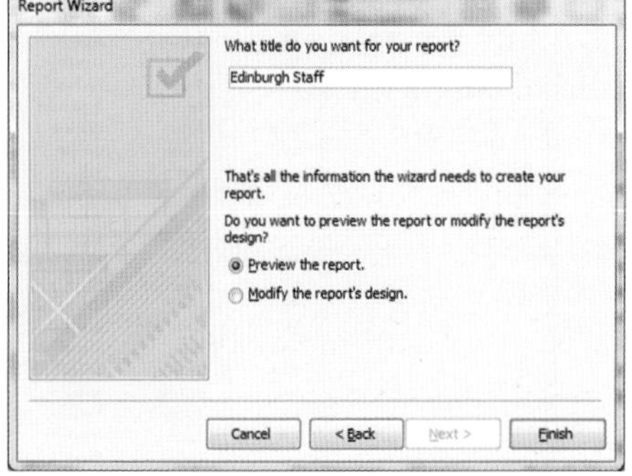

If you need to change the report heading later, you can do this by going into Design View.

The report needs to be sorted into alphabetical order of name; remember the surname is sorted first and then first name:

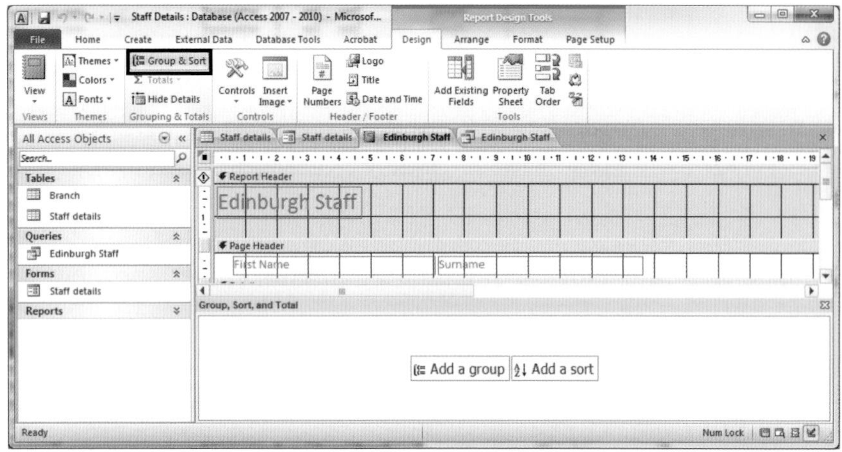

- From the Design ribbon, click Group & Sort.
- A new pane will appear at the bottom of the Design View window. Click Add a sort.
- You will be presented with a list of fields in the report. Double-click on the field you want to sort by first (Surname in this example).
- Repeat the steps for any other fields that need to be sorted (in this example we just need one more: First Name).
- Click View to view the report.

Printing

There are a few points to be aware of when printing out the different views from a database.

Printing a table or query

When printing out a table or query, it is often best practice to export into a Word® document. This makes it easier to ensure everything fits on one page and means a footer can be added.

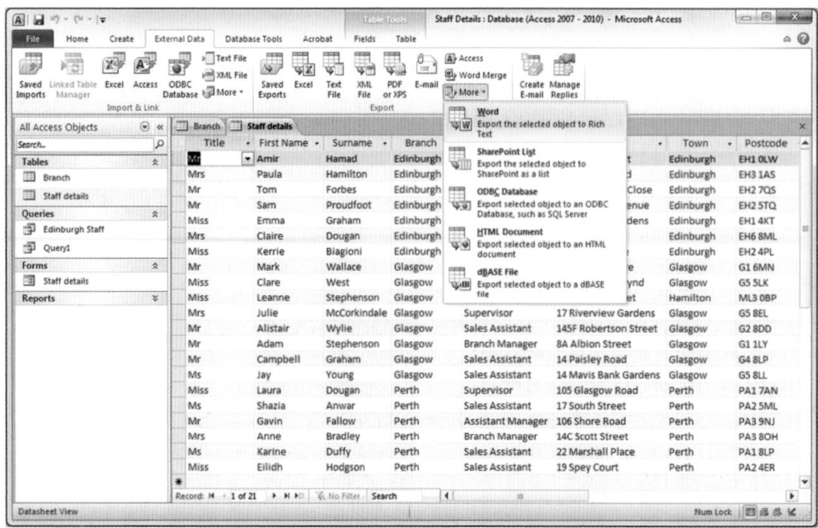

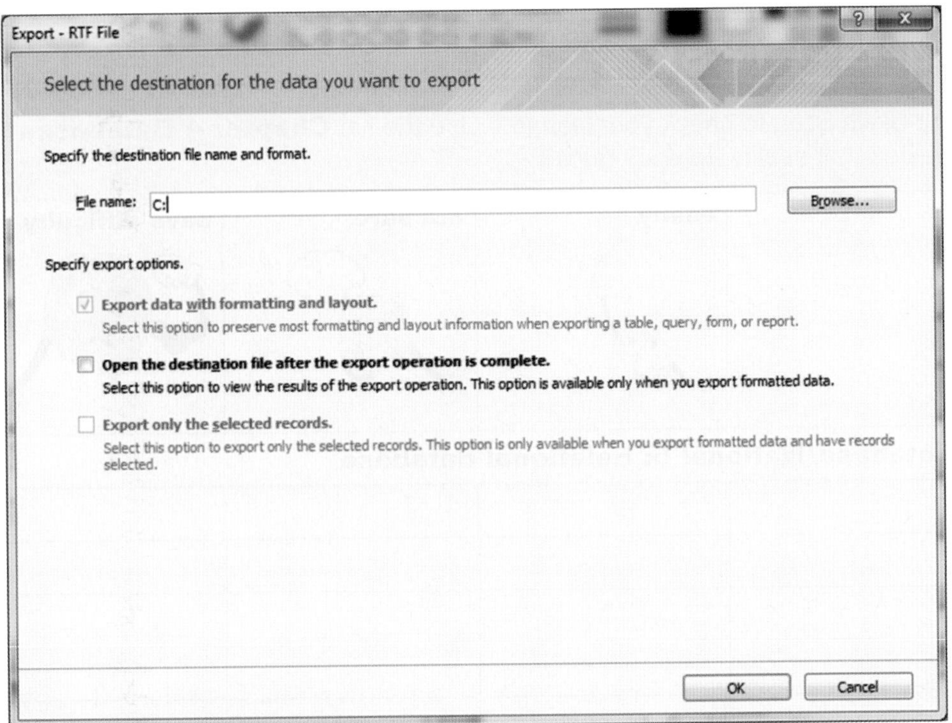

- From the External Data ribbon, select More and then click Word: Export the selected object to Rich Text.
- Click Browse and find a suitable place to save the file.
- Give the file a suitable name and click Save.
- You will be able to open the file in Word from the location you saved it.

Printing a form

Simply clicking Print, when in form view, will print every record in the database as a form. Remember, forms have been designed to view only one record at a time and it is unlikely that you will ever need to print out all records in this view. It will also clog up the printer!

Follow these steps to print one record at a time:

- Find the record you want to print by using the navigation bar at the bottom of the form.
- Click the long grey bar on the left-hand side of the form (it will turn black when it is clicked).
- Go to File > Print.
- From the Print menu, click Selected Records and click OK.

Printing a report

Reports are very simple to print: just File and Print.

> **i**
>
> The one key thing to remember when printing is to double-check all the data is visible. Sometimes columns might not be wide enough in a table or query or text boxes in the form or report not big enough.

National 4 & 5 task

Complete the following Skills Scan to check your learning. Use the file **Chapter 4 Databases Skills Scan**. Tick the box that applies to each task.

I can	**easily**	**not sure**	**have difficulty**
National 4: Flat database/National 5: Relational database			
Populate using a form			
Edit a database			
Add/delete record			
Add/delete field			
Change field names			
Alter field formats (National 5 only)			
Search database using*			
Equals =			
Greater than >			
Less than <			
And/Or (National 5 only)			
Print database – one page			
Print search – one page			
Print specific records			
Print specific fields			
Print (single) form			
Present data in a report			
Report headers/footers			
Page headers/footers			
Form headers/footers			

*N4 search and sort on ONE criteria.

N5 search and sort on TWO criteria.

IT Solutions for Administrators

Chapter 5
Use of word-processing applications to support admin tasks

By the end of this chapter you will be able to demonstrate an understanding of the purpose and uses of word processing within organisations, and develop skills in:

- ✓ creating and editing business documents
- ✓ creating, sorting and designing tables
- ✓ importing data into business documents
- ✓ merging data into business documents.

i

Organisations need to be able to produce business documents to a very high standard. Often, the first impression of a company that a customer, a supplier or a bank gets is when they receive a printed document.

There are many business documents which an Admin Assistant must work with. Here are some examples:

- letters – to customers, future employees, suppliers, banks, local authorities
- forms – for filling in either manually or electronically
- itineraries – setting out dates and times for travel arrangements
- agendas – to give information about the date, time, place and business to be discussed at a meeting
- minutes – to give information on what was discussed and decided at a meeting
- reports – to give feedback on research findings.

First let us look at a blank document and its features.

Open a new blank document and before you do anything else save it, using the filename **Introduction to WP features**.

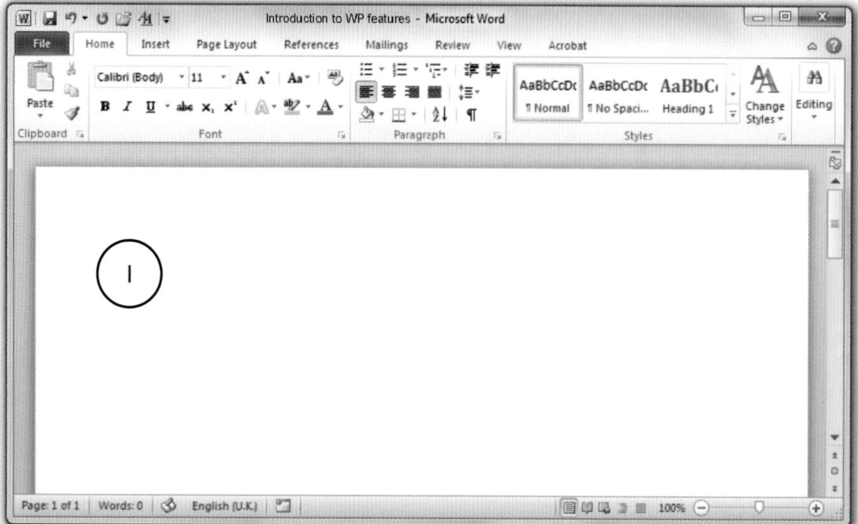

The cursor is always at the top of the blank document ready for you to start keying. To save time we will add some random text so that we can practise all of the features you need know about.

To do this simply key in the following:

- HEADING press Enter (return) twice
- =rand(2,10) press Enter (return) once

You will see two paragraphs each containing ten sentences. (You may have to put a space between the two paragraphs – depending on how the program has been set up.)

Features of word-processing documents

Select text

This can be done quickly with the shortcuts shown in Table 5.1.

Select one word	Place the cursor anywhere on the word and double-click the mouse.
Select one line	Place the cursor to the left of the line until the cursor changes to an arrow shape and single-click the mouse.
Select a paragraph	Place the cursor to the left of the paragraph until the cursor changes to an arrow shape and double-click the mouse. *or* Place the cursor anywhere in the paragraph and treble-click the mouse.
Select all text	Place the cursor to the left of the text until the cursor changes to an arrow shape and treble-click the mouse. *or* Hold the Ctrl key and press the A key.

Table 5.1

Change font and font size

You can change the font and size of a word or phrase or heading by selecting it first (remember, double-click the word). Then, using the Font menu select a different font and using the Font size menu select a bigger size, or simply click the font shortcut on the Font section of the Home ribbon.

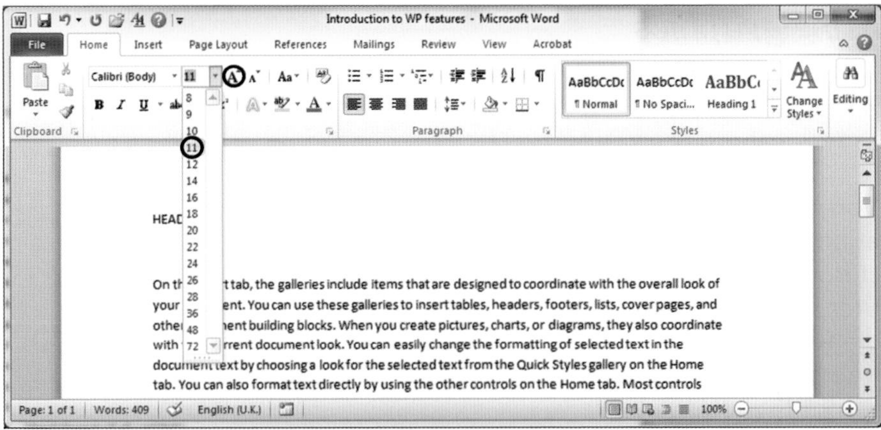

- Select the HEADING and change the font to Comic Sans, font size 18.

Use bold, italics and underline

This is often referred to as enhancing text. Select the text first (remember to use the shortcuts). Then, using the Font type menu select the shortcut on the Font section of the Home ribbon.

- Select the word 'Insert' and format to bold – B.
- Select the word 'coordinate' and format to underline – U.
- Select a sentence and format to italics – *I*.

Change line spacing, align text and set up columns

This formatting is usually applied to paragraphs or whole documents. Again the text to be changed has to be selected and the changes made using the Paragraph section of the Home ribbon and the Page Setup section of the Page Layout ribbon.

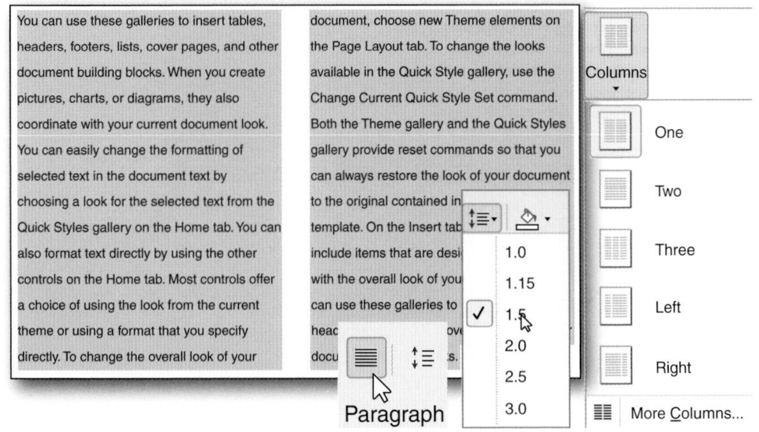

- Select the second paragraph by double-clicking the mouse in the margin (as explained in Table 5.1).
- Select Justify in the Paragraph section of the Home ribbon – or use Ctrl J.
- Select 1.5 from the Line and Paragraph Spacing section of the Home ribbon.
- Select Two Columns from the Page Setup of the Page Layout ribbon.

Inserting and formatting graphics

This can be done by adding a graphic that has already been saved in the system, such as the school badge, a photograph, a chart or a screenshot, or by using the software's own Clip Art or shapes.

- Place the cursor where you want the graphic to be placed – in this case, at the beginning of the first paragraph.
- Select Picture or Clip Art from the Illustrations section of the Insert ribbon, then search for a computer keyboard in the Search for box.
- Once you have selected and inserted the graphic, you should resize it to a proper size (that is, not too big). Always use the corner handles to do this to keep the graphic proportions the same.
- Making sure you have Wrap Text from the Arrange section of the Format ribbon, and that you have selected the graphic, click your selection.
- Select the Picture Effects section and choose a visual style you like.
- You can also change the shape of the picture by selecting the Crop to Shape option from the Crop menu.
- Try a few things for yourself.

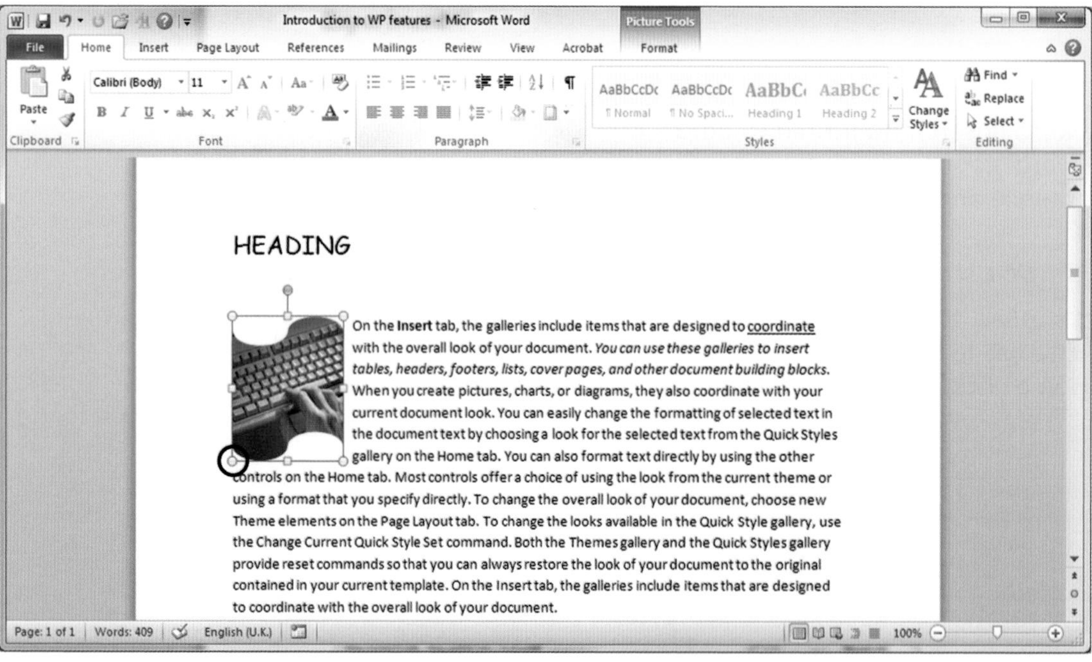

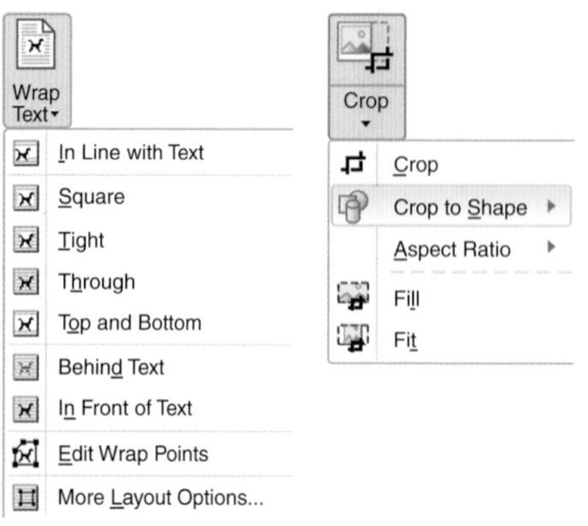

Formatting borders and shading

This is a very important feature of word processing.

- Place the cursor at the beginning of the first word of the text.
- Select the Borders and Shading option from the Paragraph section of the Home ribbon (**hint:** it is at the very bottom of the menu).
- Select the type of line, the colour and width you would like. Apply this to the top and bottom of the paragraph. Click OK.

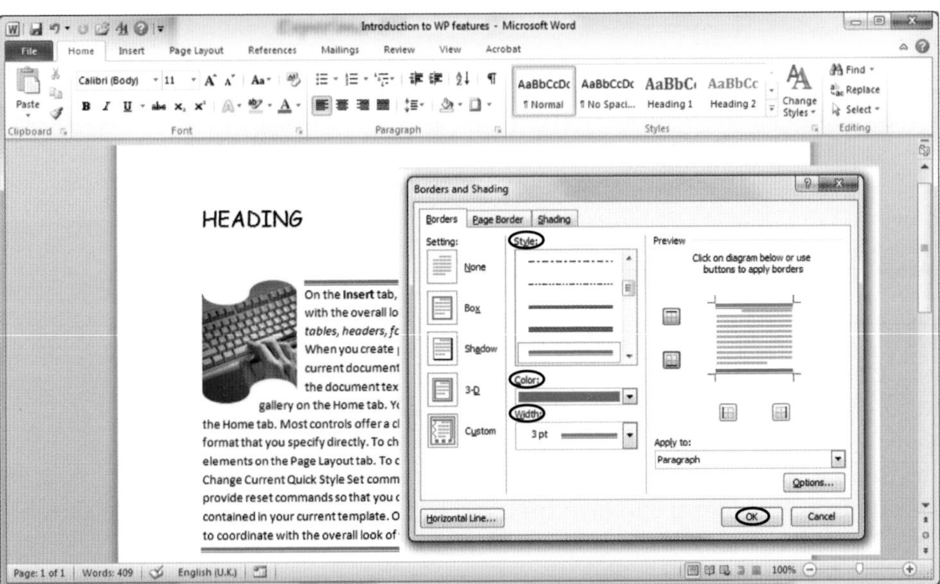

- Shading a word or paragraph is easy: Select the word/paragraph and from the Paragraph section of the Home ribbon, select the paint pot and choose a colour. Try shading a paragraph red, as below.

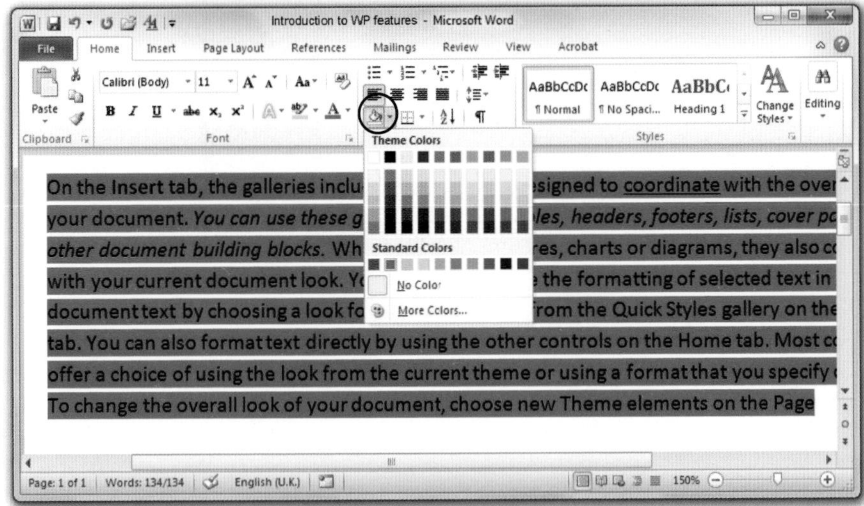

Inserting headers and footers and page numbers

It is important that you know how to use both of these features to enhance your documents.

- Find the Header & Footer section on the Insert ribbon.
- Choose Edit Header from the Header menu (you can choose one of the styles featured).

- Then choose Quick Parts on the Header & Footer section of the Insert ribbon, then Field and choose Filename from the list of options presented. (**Hint:** Key in the letter f and the Filename option will appear.)
- Click OK.

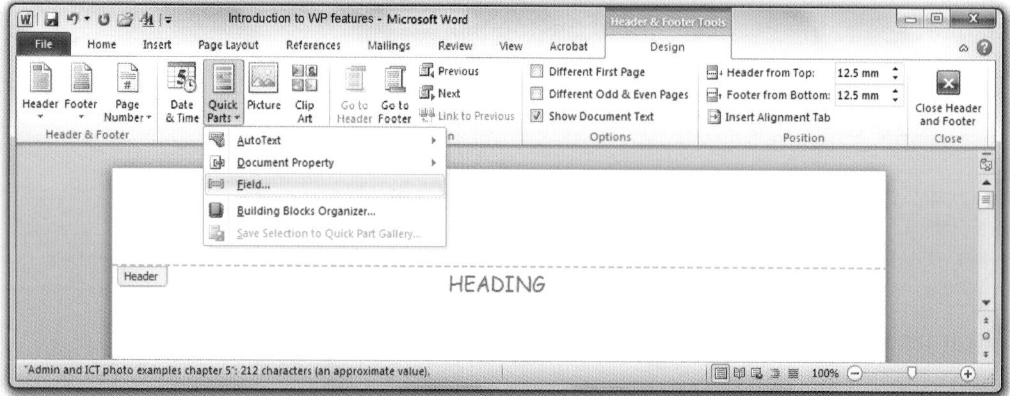

- The filename – **Introduction to WP features** – should appear automatically.
- Click Edit Footer from Footer on the ribbon, then select Date & Time from the ribbon. Decide the format you want for the date: 00/00/00 or 00/Month/0000. Click OK.
- Press Tab once to get to the middle of the Footer and select Page Number > Current position > Plain number. This menu can also be used to Format Page Numbers.

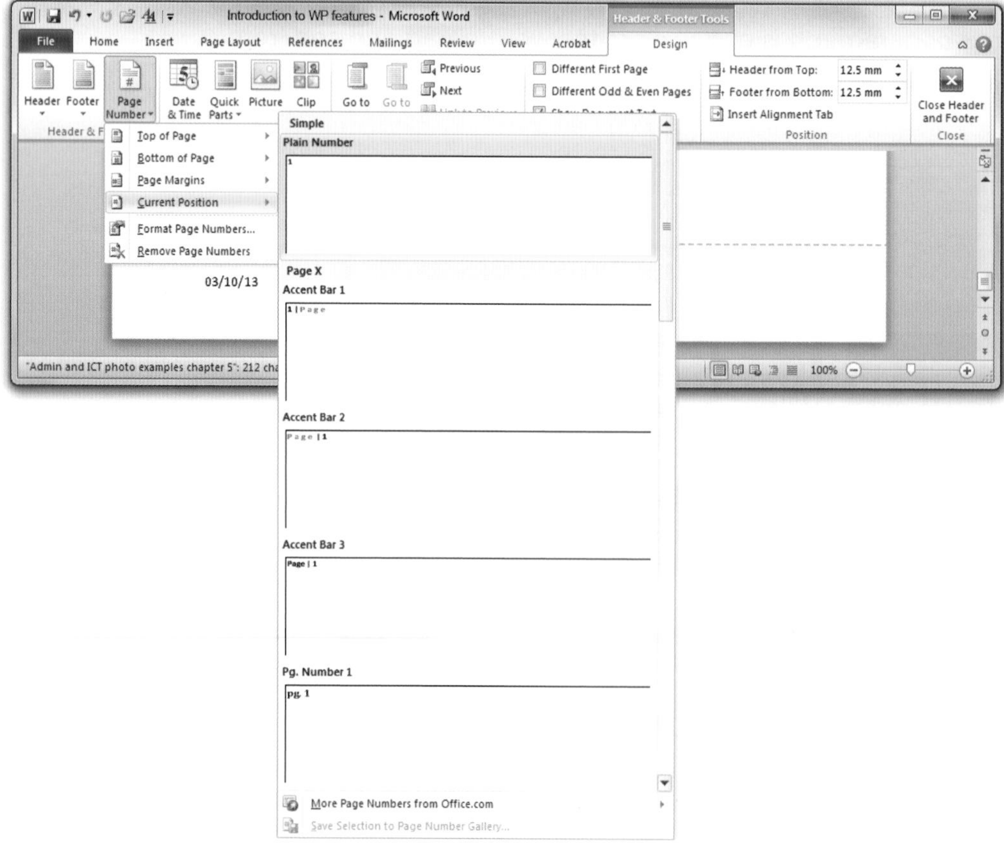

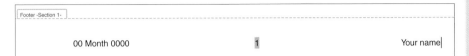

- Press Tab once more and key in your own name. Your footer should now have the date, the page number and your name displayed.

Footer -Section 1-

00 Month 0000 | 1 | Your name

> **i** You can add borders in headers and footers in the same way as for a word/paragraph/page.

Bullets and numbering

This is a very useful feature for displaying information in list format. Bullets take the form of a small graphic to the left of the information.

To practise, open a new document. Save with the filename **Bullets and Numbering Practice.**

- Key in BULLETS AND NUMBERING, then press Enter twice.
- Key in =rand(5,1) and press Enter once.
- Press Enter twice to create a space.
- Key in =rand(5,1) and press Enter once.

You should now have two sets of five separate sentences.

- Select the first set of five sentences and apply the number format (circled on Figure 5.1).
- The numbers can be moved to the left to be in line with the left margin by clicking on the Decrease Indent shortcut (circled on Figure 5.1).
- The format of the number can be changed easily by selecting the Define New Number Format option, for example the full stop can be removed or the font style, font size or font colour changed.

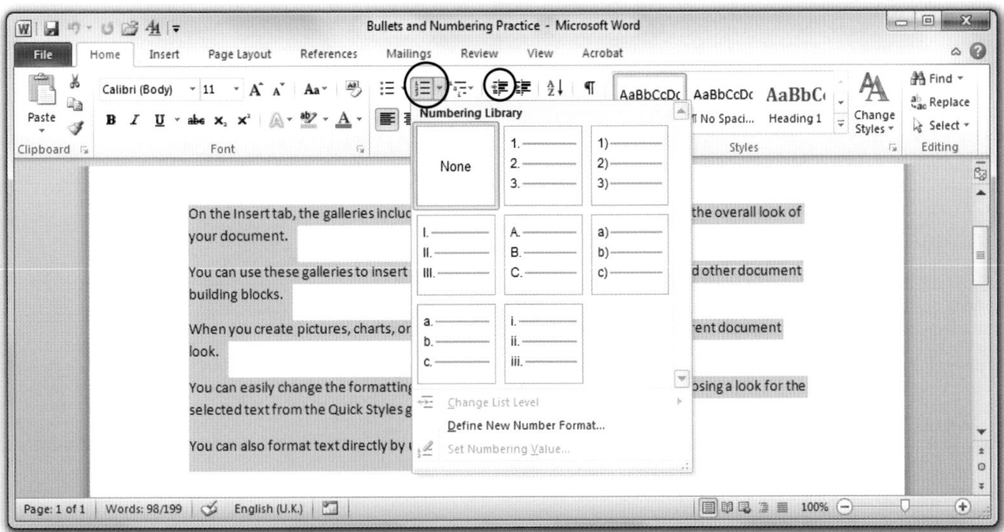

Figure 5.1

- Now select the second set of five sentences and apply the bullet format.
- The bullets can be moved in the same way as the numbers.
- The format of the bullet can be changed easily by selecting the Define New Bullet option, for example the symbol can be changed using Wingdings font, Webdings font or even using a picture.

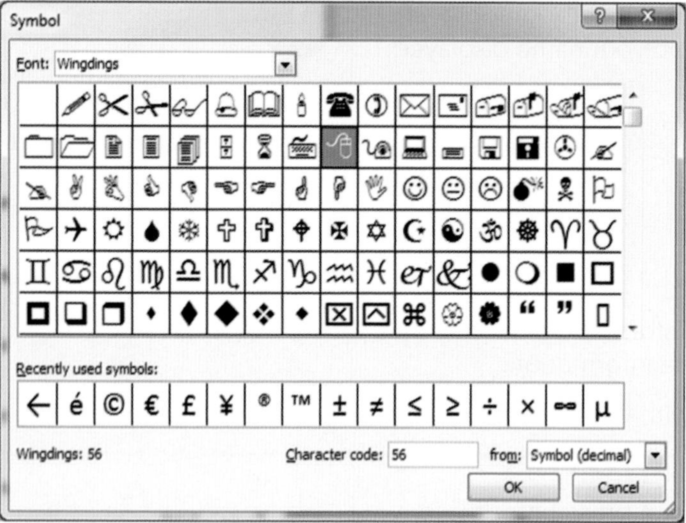

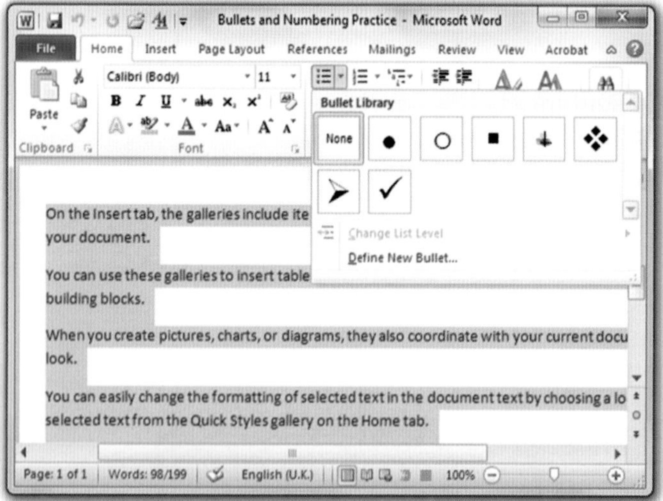

The final product can be very professional looking. You should **experiment!**

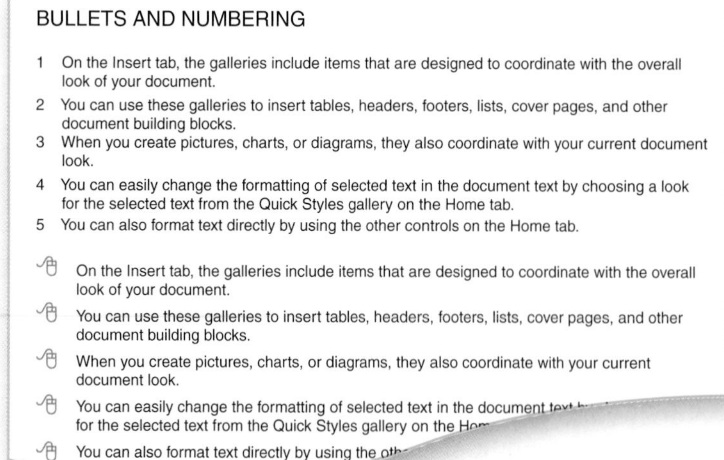

BULLETS AND NUMBERING

1 On the Insert tab, the galleries include items that are designed to coordinate with the overall look of your document.
2 You can use these galleries to insert tables, headers, footers, lists, cover pages, and other document building blocks.
3 When you create pictures, charts, or diagrams, they also coordinate with your current document look.
4 You can easily change the formatting of selected text in the document text by choosing a look for the selected text from the Quick Styles gallery on the Home tab.
5 You can also format text directly by using the other controls on the Home tab.

- On the Insert tab, the galleries include items that are designed to coordinate with the overall look of your document.
- You can use these galleries to insert tables, headers, footers, lists, cover pages, and other document building blocks.
- When you create pictures, charts, or diagrams, they also coordinate with your current document look.
- You can easily change the formatting of selected text in the document text [...] for the selected text from the Quick Styles gallery on the Ho[...]
- You can also format text directly by using the oth[...]

Tables

Creating a table in a word-processing document is a very effective way of displaying information, for example sales figures. Many Admin Assistants use tables to create labels, for mailing purposes or for name badges. Tables can also be used by Admin Assistants to gather information, for example making application forms, order forms, membership forms, staff record cards, and so on.

Tables can be formatted to look very simple or very fancy, with lots of colour and different-sized boxes. The most important thing to remember when creating a table is to think carefully about the use it will be put to for the administrative task being done.

So, let's create a simple table:

- Open a new document and save it with the filename **Table Practice**.
- Insert a Table with one row and two columns to begin with.

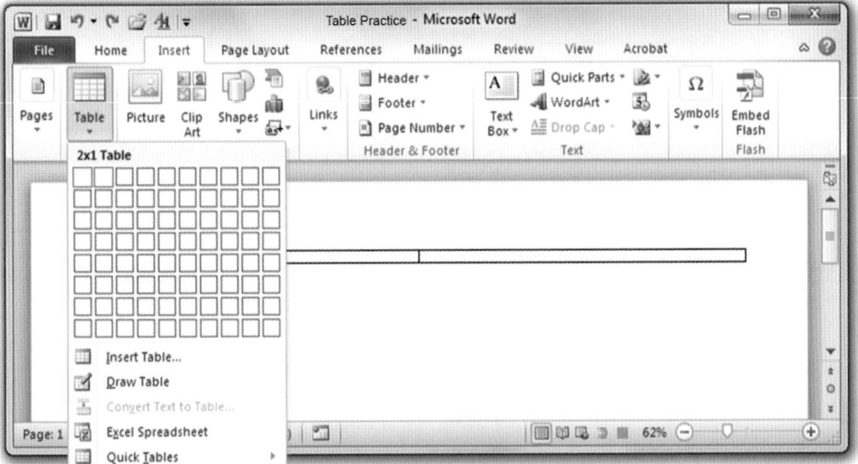

Once the table is inserted, it is easy to resize the columns by placing the mouse pointer on the column boundary you want to move until it becomes a double-headed arrow and then dragging the boundary until the column is the width you want. You can also resize the rows by placing the mouse pointer on the bottom of the row and dragging down.

It is never a good idea to use the Return key to resize the depth of the row!

It is a good idea to Show paragraph and hidden formatting symbols by clicking ¶ on the Home ribbon; this allows you to see where the text will appear.

- Reduce the size of the left column and complete the table with the information in Figure 5.2. Press Tab to add a row.

Name¤	¤
Address¤	¤
Town¤	¤
Post code¤	¤
Telephone¤	¤
Email¤	¤

Figure 5.2

- When complete, select the whole table by clicking on the Cross Hair at the top left, as shown in Figure 5.2.
- Using the Cell Alignment shortcut, select the Align Centre Left option.

You now have a very simple form which an administrator could use to collect information from new members of staff or new customers or new members of a club, and so on.

By adding graphics, resizing, merging and splitting cells (boxes) it can be made to look very different.

- Treble-clicking inside a cell will select it; it can then be easily resized

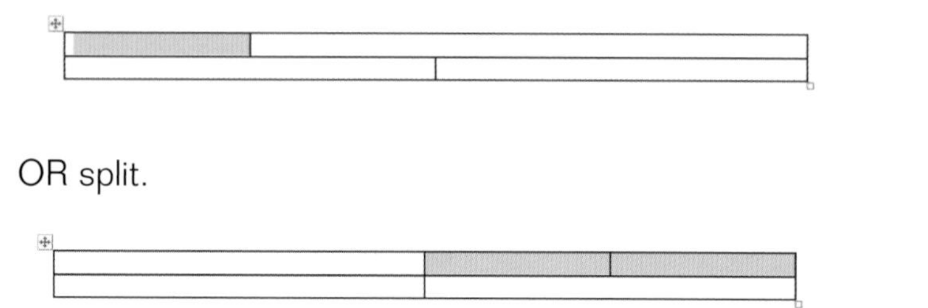

OR split.

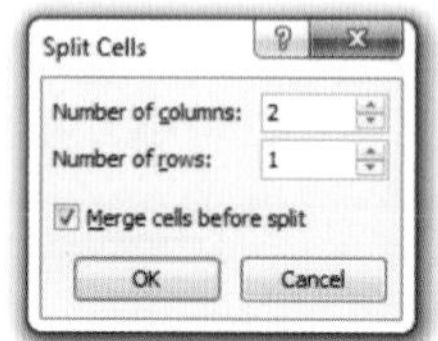

- Cells can be merged by selecting more than one cell and selecting Merge Cells from the Layout ribbon.

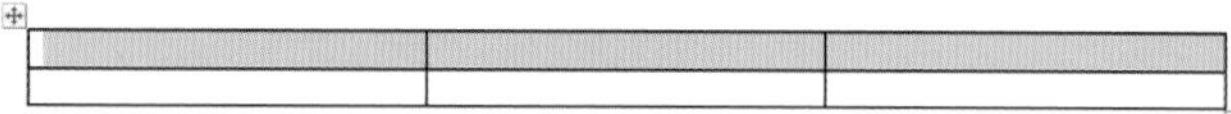

- Single cells can be split to make more columns or more rows. For example

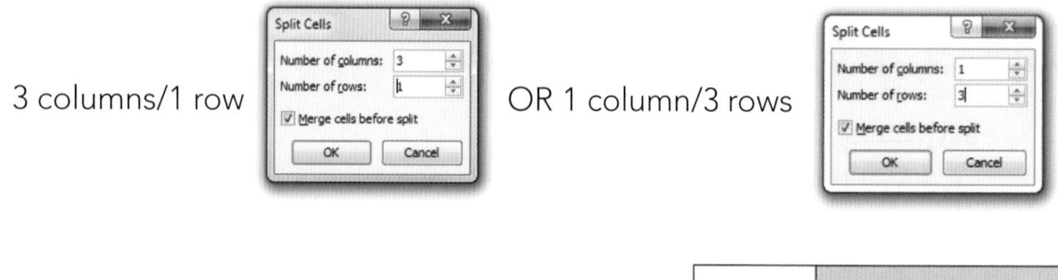

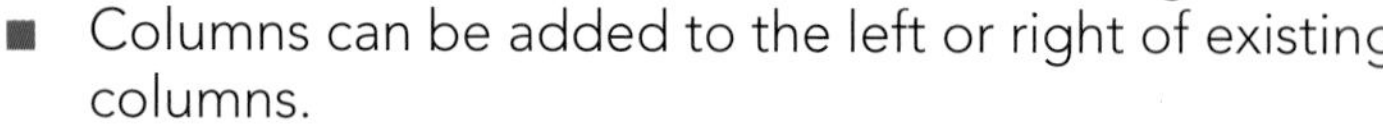

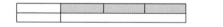

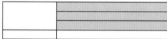

- Rows can be added above or below existing rows.
- Columns can be added to the left or right of existing columns.

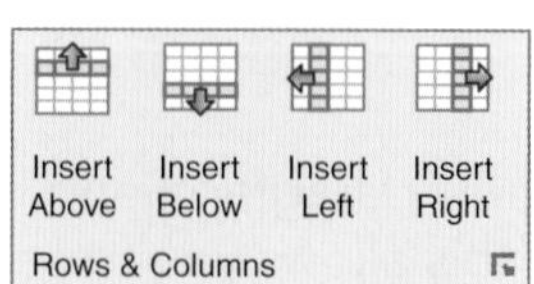

Sort — Data can be sorted by clicking anywhere within the table and selecting Sort from the Layout ribbon.

National 4 & 5 task

Create the table in Figure 5.4, making use of font sizes, alignment and graphics.

Save using the filename **Application Form**.

Company Name			
First Name		**Surname**	
Address			
Town			
Post Code			
Home Telephone			
Mobile			
Email			

Figure 5.4

National 5 task

Create the order form in Figure 5.5. Save using the filename **Order Form**.

<table>
<tr><td colspan="3">Name and Address of Customer</td><td colspan="4"></td></tr>
<tr><td colspan="3">Date of Order</td><td></td><td colspan="3" rowspan="2"></td></tr>
<tr><td colspan="3">Order Number</td><td></td></tr>
<tr><td>Catalogue Number</td><td colspan="2">Quantity</td><td>Description</td><td>Unit Cost £</td><td>VAT £</td><td>Total Cost £</td></tr>
<tr><td></td><td colspan="2"></td><td></td><td></td><td></td><td></td></tr>
<tr><td></td><td colspan="2"></td><td></td><td></td><td></td><td></td></tr>
<tr><td></td><td colspan="2"></td><td></td><td></td><td></td><td></td></tr>
<tr><td colspan="2">Signature</td><td colspan="5"></td></tr>
</table>

Figure 5.5

Business letter

Most business letters have a formal layout as they are usually sent from an organisation to a customer or another organisation. All business letters must be accurate, with no spelling or keying-in errors. They are usually printed on headed paper which the business has designed. This headed paper usually contains the contact details of the business and a graphic or logo which is appropriate to the type of business.

Most businesses have their headed paper specially printed and simply put the special paper into the printer paper tray as and when required.

Some firms do not have specially printed paper but have an electronic copy saved on the network to be used when required. Figure 5.6 shows an example of what headed paper might look like.

Name of Business

Address
Town
Postcode

Telephone: 01234 567890

www.companyname.co.uk

Figure 5.6

National 4 & 5 task

Create your own version of a letterhead using different sizes of the same font. Use an appropriate graphic. Save using the filename **Letterhead**.

Figure 5.7 is an example of a business letter using the normal layout that most businesses use.

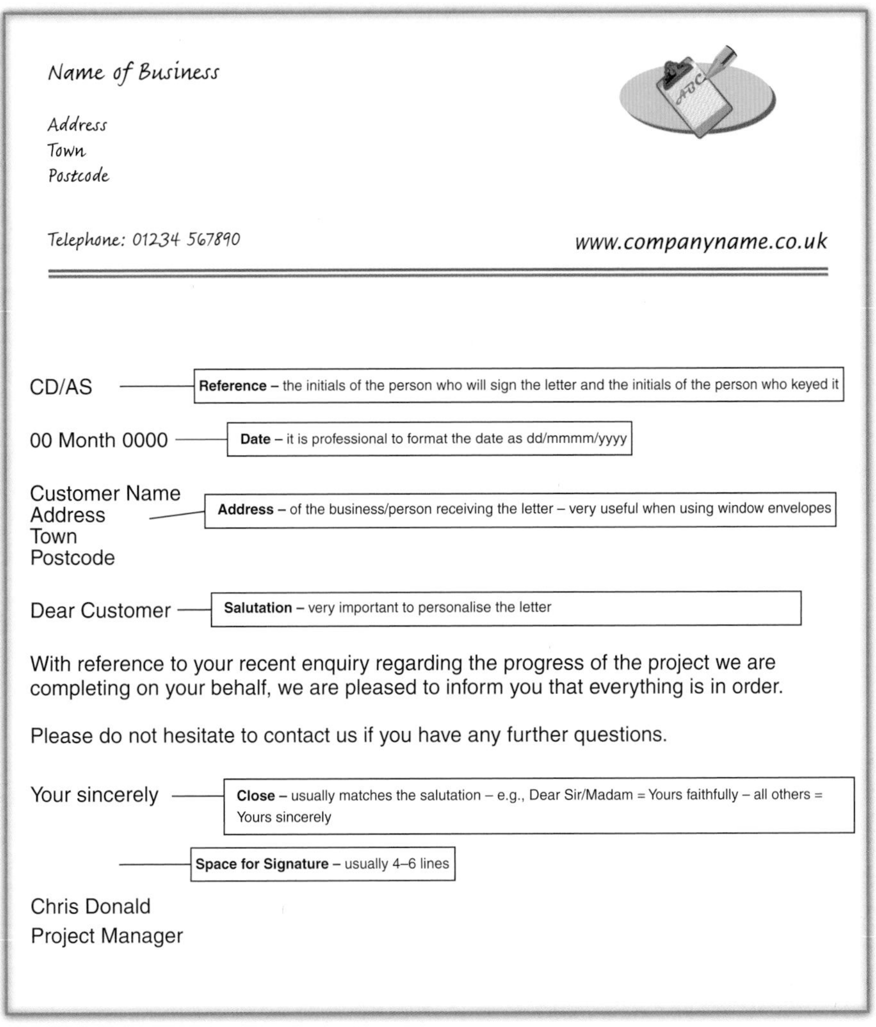

Name of Business

Address
Town
Postcode

Telephone: 01234 567890 www.companyname.co.uk

CD/AS — **Reference** – the initials of the person who will sign the letter and the initials of the person who keyed it

00 Month 0000 — **Date** – it is professional to format the date as dd/mmmm/yyyy

Customer Name
Address — **Address** – of the business/person receiving the letter – very useful when using window envelopes
Town
Postcode

Dear Customer — **Salutation** – very important to personalise the letter

With reference to your recent enquiry regarding the progress of the project we are completing on your behalf, we are pleased to inform you that everything is in order.

Please do not hesitate to contact us if you have any further questions.

Your sincerely — **Close** – usually matches the salutation – e.g., Dear Sir/Madam = Yours faithfully – all others = Yours sincerely

Space for Signature – usually 4–6 lines

Chris Donald
Project Manager

Figure 5.7

National 4 & 5 task

Open the standard letter file **Interview Invitation** and complete with the information in Figure 5.8.

Print one copy of the letter ready for signature and posting – no need for an envelope or label as the letter will be sent using a window envelope.

Delete all comments and save using the filename **B Pearson Interview**.

Information for interview
Name Miss Bethany Pearson
Address 45 Newhome Street G35 8KL
Date Wednesday – next week – you will need to find the actual date for me – thanks
Time 1100 hours
Place R207 on the first floor

Figure 5.8

Mail merge

Sometimes the same letter is sent to more than one person. Rather than creating and editing individual letters, it is a better idea to use mail merge. This is easily done with a standard letter and merging the individual information using a table. Tables can be created from a database (by exporting information selected from records to a word-processing document) or if there are no records, for example when selecting candidates for a job from an application form, by simply creating a table with the information required.

Prospective candidates

Title	Name 1	Name 2	Address	Town	PC	Date	Time	Place
Miss	Bethany	Pearson	45 Newhome Street	Glasgow	G35 8KL	00 Month 0000	1100 hours	R207 on first floor
Mr	Chris	Wilson	123 Glasgow Road	East Kilbride	G74 4HG	00 Month 0000	1300 hours	R101 on ground floor

Table 5.2

- Open the file Interview Invitation and complete the mail merge as follows, using the file (Table 5.2) Prospective candidates for interview.
- Complete the Reference and Date section.
- From the Mailing ribbon, Select Recipients, Use Existing List …
- From the Insert Merge Field menu, insert the necessary fields.

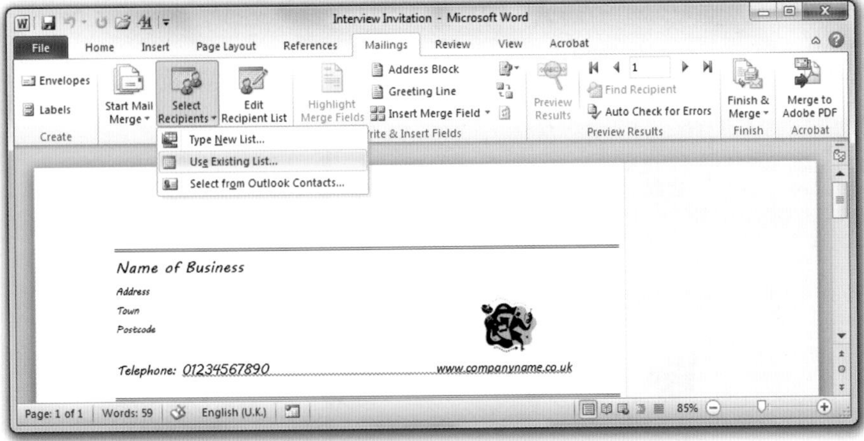

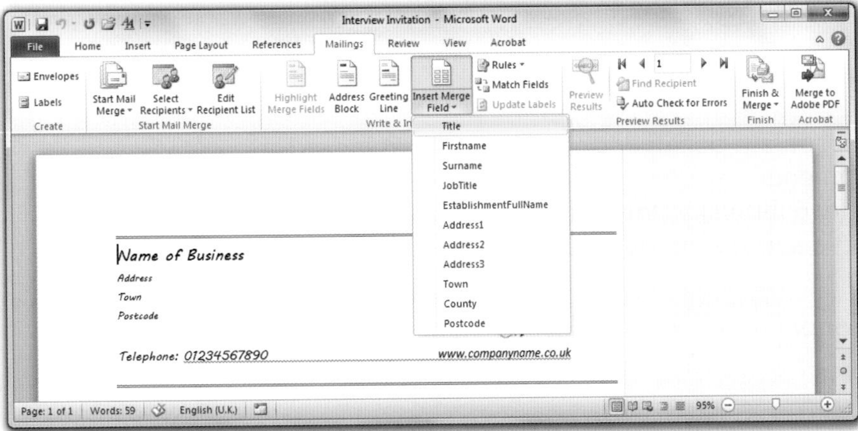

When completed the merge information should look like the shaded areas.

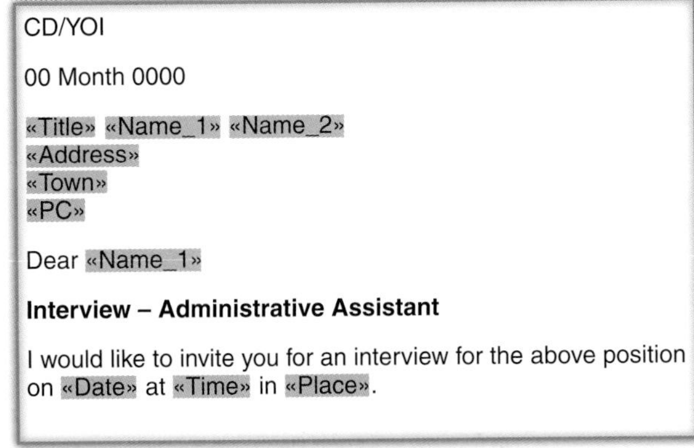

CD/YOI

00 Month 0000

«Title» «Name_1» «Name_2»
«Address»
«Town»
«PC»

Dear «Name_1»

Interview – Administrative Assistant

I would like to invite you for an interview for the above position on «Date» at «Time» in «Place».

Insert a space between each merge field so they will not be joined up when you merge.

Print a copy of the letter showing the Merge Fields.

- Select **Preview** Results. It is the same procedure for two records as it is for 200!

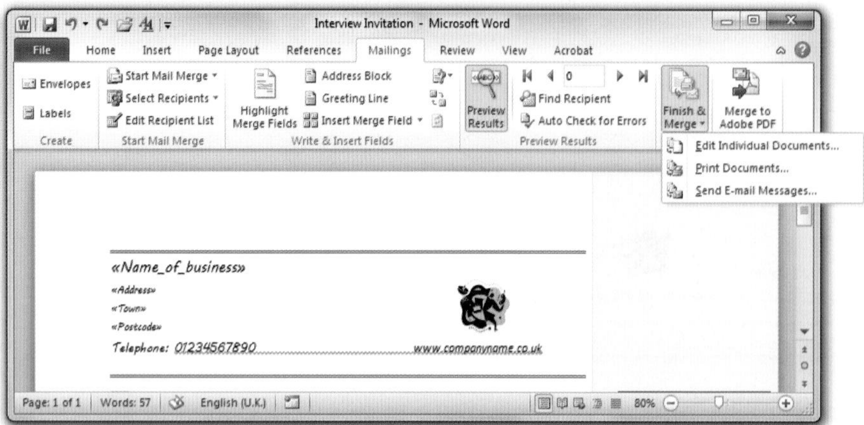

Once you have merged the two documents you can:

- Finish & Merge to a new separate document by selecting Edit Individual Documents *or* Print Documents.
- Save the new document (two letters) as **Interview letters completed**.
- It is also possible to select a specific merged document using the ◀ arrow ▶ keys to navigate/find it.

The final document – ready for printing – should show the merged information as shaded areas.

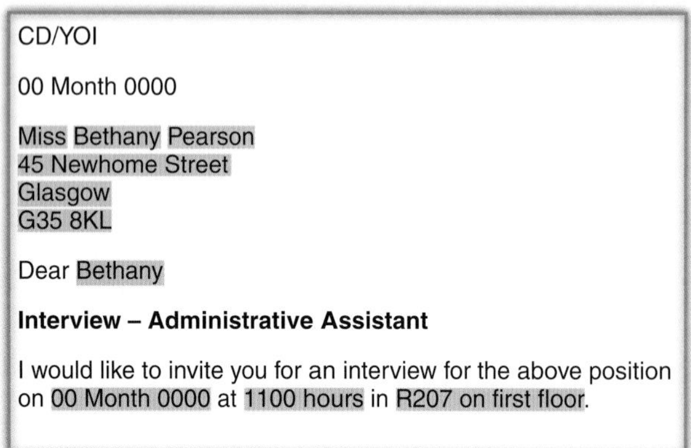

CD/YOI

00 Month 0000

Miss Bethany Pearson
45 Newhome Street
Glasgow
G35 8KL

Dear Bethany

Interview – Administrative Assistant

I would like to invite you for an interview for the above position on 00 Month 0000 at 1100 hours in R207 on first floor.

- Print both letters.

Many companies have **standard documents** on file and some use a 'bank' of sentences that can be used to produce standard documents. This is so that all correspondence leaving the firm or used within the firm is of a similar style, font, layout, and so on. These are usually saved on an **internal network**, available to all staff, and are often referred to as **templates**.

Integrate information

Word-processing documents can be **integrated** with other documents and files. It is easy to copy and paste anything that is on file, for example a chart, spreadsheet data, the results of a search in a database or even text from another word-processing document.

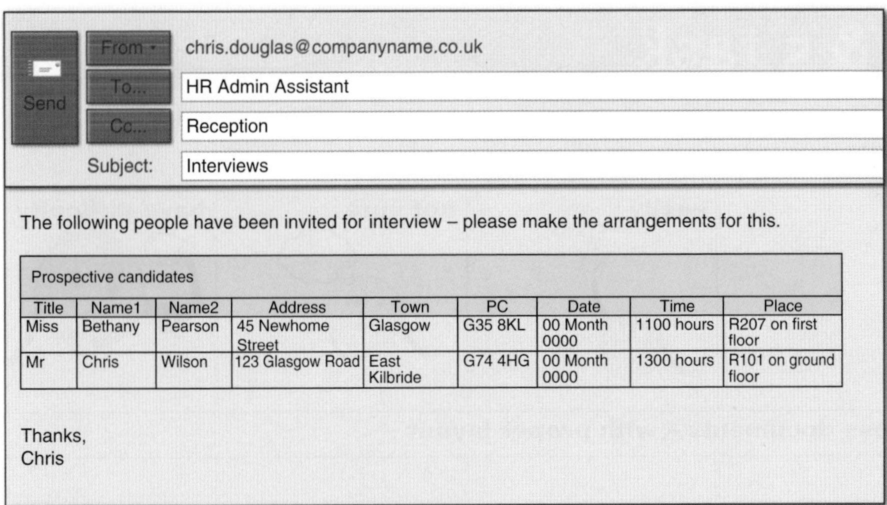

From: chris.douglas@companyname.co.uk
To: HR Admin Assistant
Cc: Reception
Subject: Interviews

The following people have been invited for interview – please make the arrangements for this.

Prospective candidates

Title	Name1	Name2	Address	Town	PC	Date	Time	Place
Miss	Bethany	Pearson	45 Newhome Street	Glasgow	G35 8KL	00 Month 0000	1100 hours	R207 on first floor
Mr	Chris	Wilson	123 Glasgow Road	East Kilbride	G74 4HG	00 Month 0000	1300 hours	R101 on ground floor

Thanks,
Chris

The simplest method of integrating data is to use Copy and Paste between the two files. However, sometimes it is necessary to link the two files so that if any data changes in the data being integrated it will automatically be updated in the original document.

This is easily done as follows:

- Copy the text as normal.
- Select Paste Special (don't just paste).
- Select Paste link.
- Changes to the source files will be changed in your document.

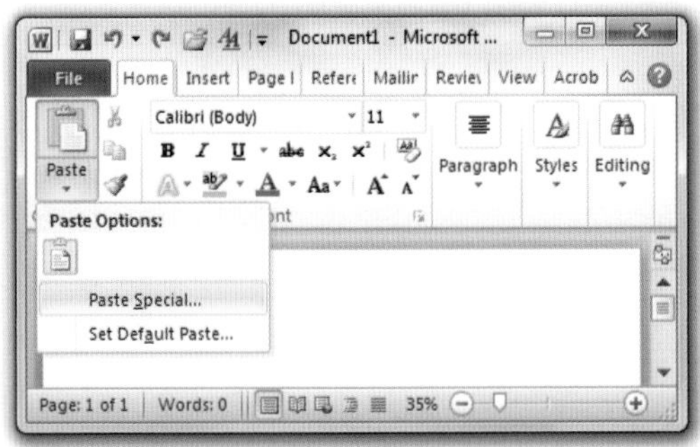

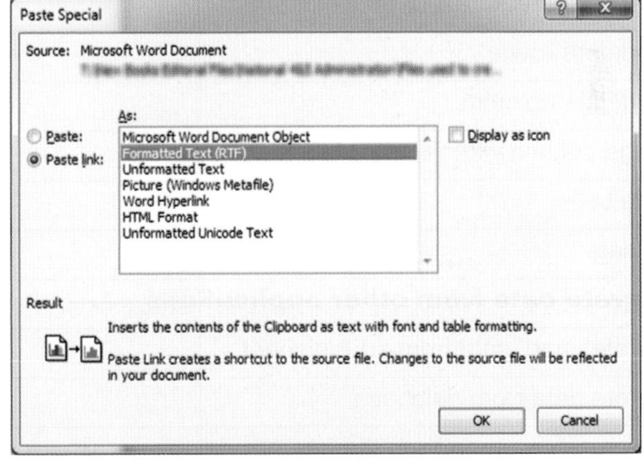

Many business documents are handwritten in the first instance. These documents invariably contain errors – in spelling and sentence construction. Any changes to be made to these documents can be indicated by the use of special correction signs called manuscript corrections (*see Appendix*).

It is a good idea to have a routine for keying-in the text on paper copies to ensure complete accuracy. Before you begin you should:

- Read through the whole document quickly to make sure you understand it.
- Check the spelling of any unusual names or terminology.
- Know the layouts and rules required for business documents you are creating or editing.

National 4 & 5 task

Complete the following Skills Scan to check your learning. Use the file **Chapter 5 Word-processing Skills Scan**. Tick the box that applies to each task.

I can	**easily**	**not sure**	**have difficulty**
Create and edit business documents – with proper layout			
Change font and size			
Change margins			
Use bold/italics/underline			
Align/justify text			
Insert/format graphics			
Use bullets and numbering			
Insert headers and footers			
Insert borders/shading			
Insert page numbers			
Create a table			
Insert/delete/edit text			
Add/delete rows			
Add/delete columns			
Change column widths			
Shade cells			
Sort data*			
Integrate data from other applications			
Integrate chart/data from spreadsheet			
Integrate data from database			
Integrate information from the internet			
Integrate text from another file			
Print document			
National 5 only: Create a table			
Insert formula			
Split/merge cells			
National 5 only: Integrate data from other applications			
Merge data			
Print merge fields			

*N4 sort on ONE criteria.
N5 sort on TWO criteria.

Unit 3

Communication in Administration

Chapter 6

Searching and sourcing information

By the end of this chapter you will be able to demonstrate an understanding of:

- ✓ searching for and extracting/downloading relevant information from the intranet or internet
- ✓ using search engines and navigating hyperlinks
- ✓ copying/printing extracts of information.

In addition at National 5 level, you will:

- ✓ be able to evaluate the features of reliable sources of information
- ✓ understand the consequences of using unreliable information.

An Admin Assistant may be asked to find information for others working in an organisation. Technology has transformed the way information is sourced.

The types of information an Admin Assistant needs to find and use on a regular basis could be:

- documents and files kept electronically for use within the organisation
- templates of standard documents to be used for internal and external communication
- electronic diary information to arrange meetings.

And sometimes less often:

- travel information, for example train timetables, flight information, hotels and accommodation
- marketing information to help sell more products
- up-to-date news, for example traffic, weather, and so on.

Most organisations will have access to all of this type of information and much more.

Intranet

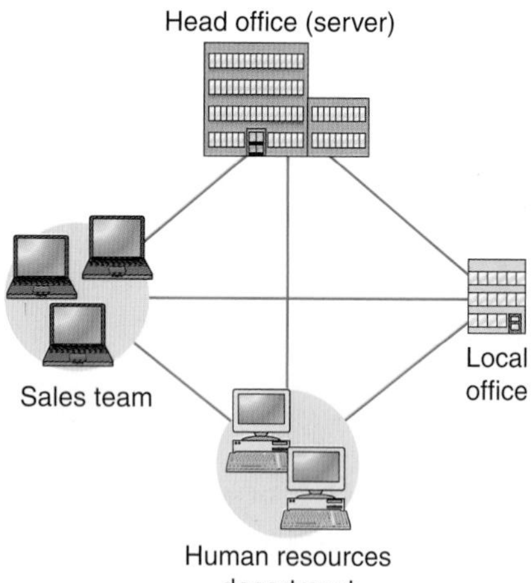

Information which is for the exclusive use of an organisation is normally stored on an internal network or **intranet**. An intranet is where all electronic sources of information are stored and is a collection of private computer networks within the organisation. An intranet uses network technologies to enable communication between people or work groups to take place. It also helps improve the data-sharing capability of an organisation's employees.

Intranet = network + information resources + information services

An intranet can run over a local area network (LAN) where only staff in the same building can use it, or it can run over a wide area network (WAN) where staff from around the world can log in.

Both of these systems require the use of a user name or log-in.

Many schools and organisations use intranets. The simplest form of intranet consists of an internal email system and perhaps a message-board service. However, more sophisticated intranets include:

- internal web pages containing up-to-date internal information
- notices for staff
- daily bulletin information
- forms for staff use, for example holiday-request forms, travel/accommodation request forms, and so on.
- documents, spreadsheets, presentations and databases
- personnel information, for example name, department, job title, telephone extension number, and so on.

Features of an intranet include:

- fast, easy and low cost to set up
- easy to learn and use
- can be easily connected with other systems
- use of multimedia so it is visually pleasing and can include hypertext links to assist with easy navigation between the internal web pages
- improved communication by incorporation of news boards, message boards, pop-up warnings, and so on.
- storage and sharing of knowledge and internal information.

- People should only be able to view and/or download information appropriate to their job; an intranet structure shouldn't allow everyone in the organisation access to everything! *(See page 12.)*
- Remote access to the intranet by staff members when at home or travelling increases the risk of hacking into the system.
- Staff members should change their passwords regularly.
- IT staff should regularly check for viruses.

The purpose of the intranet is to help employees with their work and it is the responsibility of the organisation to ensure that dedicated staff are employed to keep things running smoothly.

Internet

The **internet** is a computer network that connects computers worldwide. The internet is used for many things, such as email, online chat, news services, forums and the World Wide Web (WWW), which contains websites, web pages, blogs, and so on. Sometimes an Admin Assistant is required to find and download information from external sources. The use of the internet makes this very easy to do. This makes the organisation of events (see Chapter 2) much more effective. The features of the internet are very similar to the features of an intranet, that is, web pages linked by **hyperlinks** containing information.

Anyone can create and upload a website; no permission is required! This can be very difficult to deal with and it is the responsibility of the Admin Assistant to ensure that any information sourced from an internet website is evaluated for:

- reliability, e.g. factual information regarding a visiting speaker
- accuracy of detail, e.g. timetables need to be up to date when planning travel
- security of website, e.g. cannot be edited by unauthorised personnel
- risk of downloading a virus.

It is also important to consider if the website chosen is:

- user-friendly and easy to navigate, e.g. does the website have a good search facility?
- an established well-known website which is universally recognised and trusted.

Read the following case study which highlights the problems of using an unknown and possibly unreliable website.

Case study – ABC Enterprises

Every day the Admin Assistant, Chris, receives many emails from different companies offering special travel deals. One of these emails is from a company called Trusty Travel, which claims to offer cheap travel and accommodation for business executives. Chris follows the hyperlink provided and immediately signs up to get access to the special-offer details, entering lots of information about the company, including banking and credit card details, as he does so.

The next day Sonja Kerr, Sales Manager, asks Chris to book a flight to New York for the following Monday morning. Of course, Chris remembers that he has signed up to this website and books a flight and forwards the email confirmation to Sonja.

The following Monday, Chris receives a phone call from Sonja informing him that there is no such flight! Chris revisits the website used and discovers that he cannot contact them by phone, or even write to them, as the only contact on the website is the email address.

Sonja is forced to book an expensive ticket to travel on the next available flight, which is not until much later in the day.

What should Chris have done?

- ✓ Chris should always *follow company policy* regarding issuing confidential information to new suppliers, especially on websites.
- ✓ Before using a new supplier, Chris should have *confirmed all details provided* on the website by contacting the company personally – either by telephone or in writing.
- ✓ Chris should always check websites for security promises:
    1. check for 'https' in the prefix of the web page address; this means that it is a secure website
    2. click on the lock icon in the status bar of the browser, again to check that it is secure.
- ✓ Chris should check reviews of any new site; there are many people who will post information regarding companies, especially rogue companies.

What are the consequences of Chris' actions?

- × Cost:
    - The company has been charged for a ticket that does not exist!
    - An additional ticket had to be bought, which would have been very expensive as it was a last-minute purchase.
- × Sonja will be late for her meeting in New York, and may even miss it, which could mean the company loses business.
- × The reputation of ABC Enterprises could be severely damaged and future business with other companies could be put at risk.
- × All banking information and credit cards may have to be stopped and replacements requested from the bank.
- × The internal network may be compromised; a virus may have infected the internal network of the company.
- × Chris could face disciplinary procedures, which could result in the loss of his job!

Unit 3

Communication in Administration

Chapter 7

Communicating information using DTP and presentation applications

By the end of this chapter you will be able to demonstrate an understanding of:

- ✓ **skills in creating and editing professional documents using desktop publishing software**
- ✓ **skills in creating and editing professional multi-media presentations.**

One of the many tasks expected of an Admin Assistant is to prepare posters and presentations to communicate information to other members of staff or customers and callers. There are many methods of communication available and the Admin Assistant must aim for accuracy and clarity of the information contained in any document.

There are many ways of presenting information for others to read or keep for future reference, either printed or electronically.

- Spreadsheet software can be used to create graphs and charts which make numerical information extremely easy to understand.
- Database software can be used to create reports containing specific data in a condensed format.
- Word-processing software can be used to prepare other business documents such as letters, mailing labels, forms, reports and itineraries, all of which are very important to the smooth running of any office.

Desktop publishing

Sometimes Admin Assistants are required to produce posters and leaflets to communicate or display important information. Because these documents contain important information, it is essential that they have a professional finish. The best way to achieve a professional finish is by using **desktop publishing** (DTP) techniques. This can be done using a dedicated software package such as Microsoft Publisher®.

Publisher® contains a lot of 'wizard/ready-made' type publications which pre-design the document, for example a newsletter. This contains a lot of textboxes and graphics (known as placeholders). It can also be formatted into columns, and so on. All that needs to be done is to replace the text and graphics with your own relevant text and graphics.

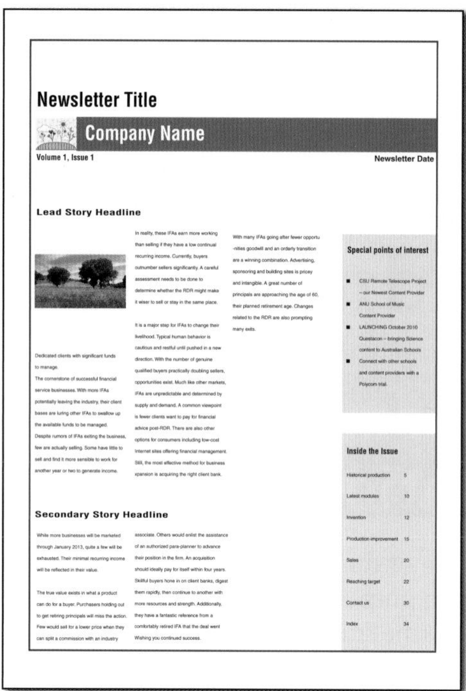

The wizards are called 'templates'. There are many different templates available, as you can see in Figure 7.1.

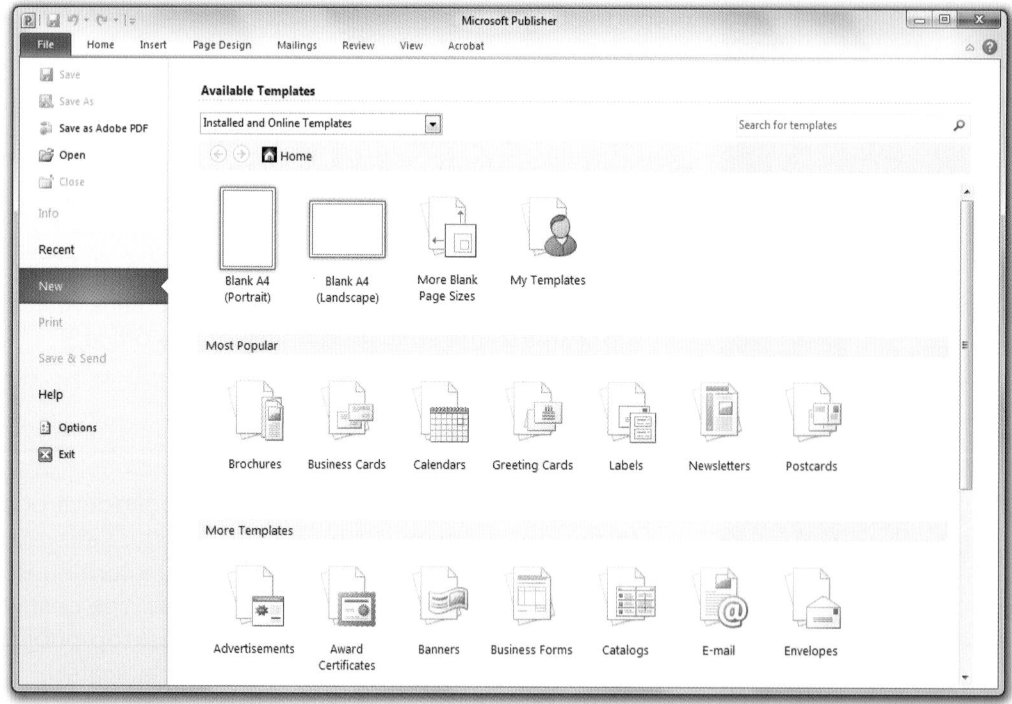

Figure 7.1

The templates are categorised in groups, for example brochures, business cards, labels, and so on and they are mostly designed for businesses to use. They can be set up to include the company name, address and any other relevant contact information automatically. However, most modern word-processing software packages can also produce equally professional-looking documents.

DTP is a mixture of text and graphics so that information is displayed in an interesting and visually attractive manner.

Making an attractive poster using word-processing software

Let's create a poster using Word.

- Open a new blank document.
- Save the document with the filename **Practice Poster**.
- Select Landscape layout.

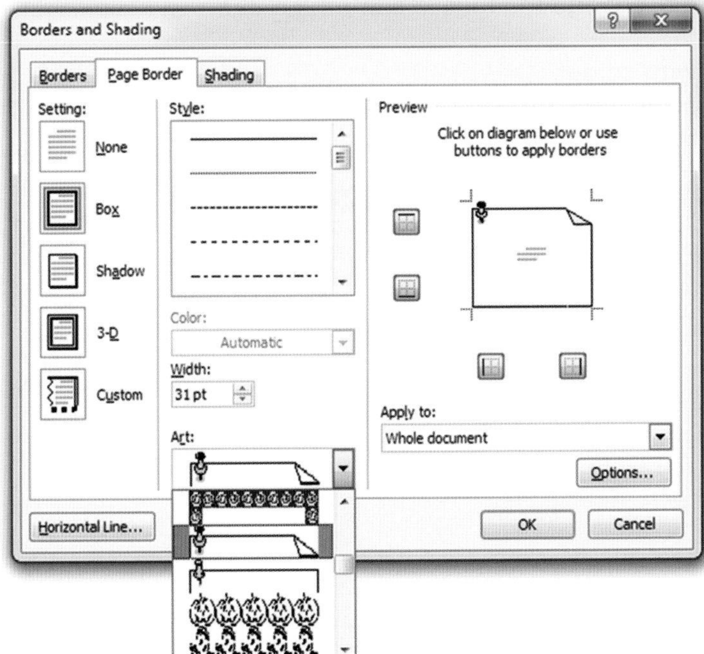

- From the Page Background section of the Page Layout ribbon select a page border. You can choose the type of border: box, shadow, and so on.
- You can choose different styles of line and change the width of the line to suit the poster.
- You can also choose Clip Art and pictures, as we did in chapter 5, again changing the size of the art to suit the poster.

Graphics

You can insert pictures (already saved), shapes, Clip Art, SmartArt, charts, screenshots and WordArt to enhance the look of a document to make it look more professional.

Top tip: When producing a poster, it is a good idea to view the whole page while creating the work; remember: a poster needs to be seen from a distance.

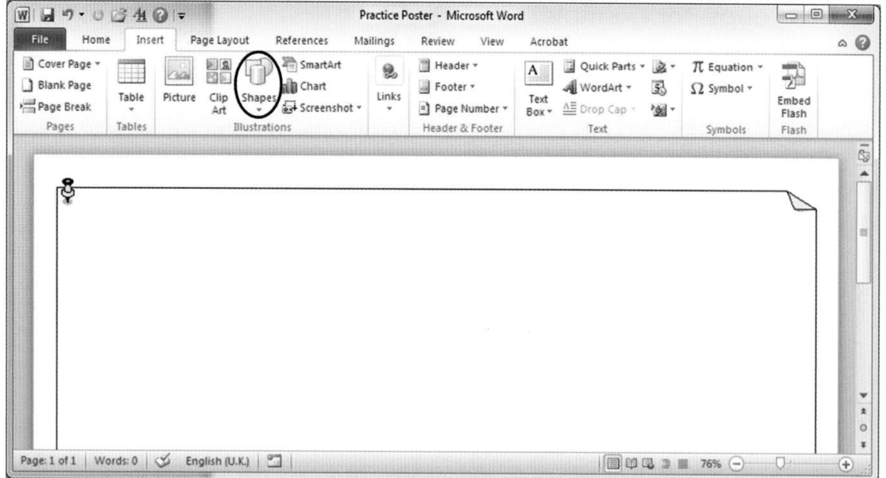

You can also use text boxes to insert text wherever you want it to appear.

- Insert a textbox. Key in the word Notice, change the font to something eye-catching and increase the font size.
- Remove the Outline and Fill the box with colour.
- Rotate the box slightly for a more effective look by grabbing the green circle with the mouse and turning to the left.

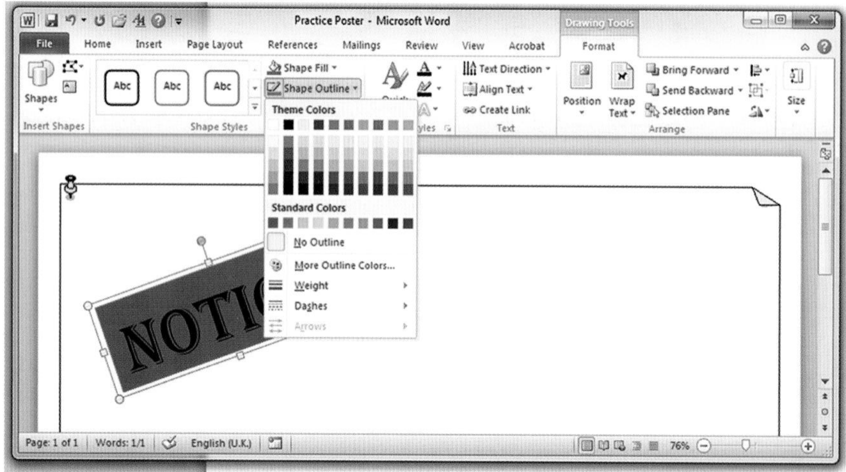

- Insert another textbox and key in the following text:
  The monthly Committee Meeting will take place in the Conference Room at 1000 hours on the first Tuesday of the month.
- Change the font to make it stand out; it should take up at least half of the page. Make use of centre alignment for the time and place to make it easy to read.
- Insert an explosion shape from the Stars and Banners section of the Shapes.
- This shape is like a text box and so text can be easily added. Key in the following text:
  Please check your email for the Agenda.
- Enlarge the font size and change the font to match the second text box. Choose a colour for the shape and one for the font. Rotate this explosion shape to enhance its effectiveness.
- The final poster should look something like Figure 7.2. Print a copy of this poster or email it to your teacher.

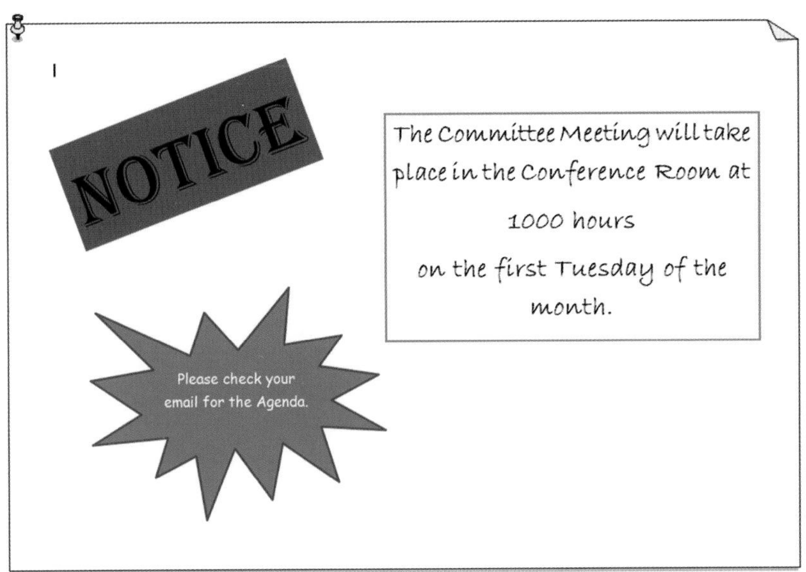

Figure 7.2

There are many DTP features within word-processing software. You should **experiment!**

National 4 & 5 task

Make a poster to inform everyone that a visiting speaker from Mary's Meals will be visiting next Monday at lunchtime. Everyone is welcome. Insert a suitable graphic and ensure the information is easy to read. Print the poster or email it to your teacher.

Making an attractive leaflet using word-processing software

- Open a new blank document.
- Save the document with the filename **Practice A4 Leaflet**.
- From the Pages section of the Page SetUp, select Book fold.
- Key in the following text on the first page:
  Front Page
- Increase the font size to **72**.
- Insert a graphic; choose a clipboard from Clip Art.
- From the Page Layout, select Break > Section Break, *not page break.*
- On the next page (inside left) key in **=rand(1,10)**.
- Insert another page break (page 3) and key in **=rand(4,1)**.
- From the Page Layout, select Break > Section Break, *not page break.*
- Using WordArt, choose a style and key in Back Page on page 4. Resize, rotate and transform the text to make it more attractive.

Pages
Multiple pages: Normal
Normal
Mirror margins
2 pages per sheet
Book fold
Preview

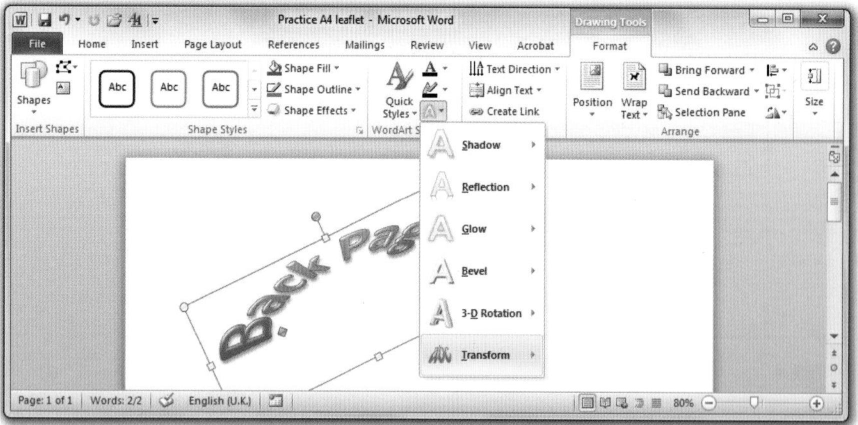

- Format page 2 into two columns (remember to select all the text on this page).
- Format page 3 into bullets; increase the font size and select an interesting symbol for the bullets.
- On pages 2 and 3, insert a footer with the following text: **Prepared by (your own name)**
- Print the leaflet on one A4 sheet back-to-back.

Your final leaflet should look something like Figure 7.3.

> **Top tip:** When displaying text in an A4 leaflet it is a good idea to justify text.

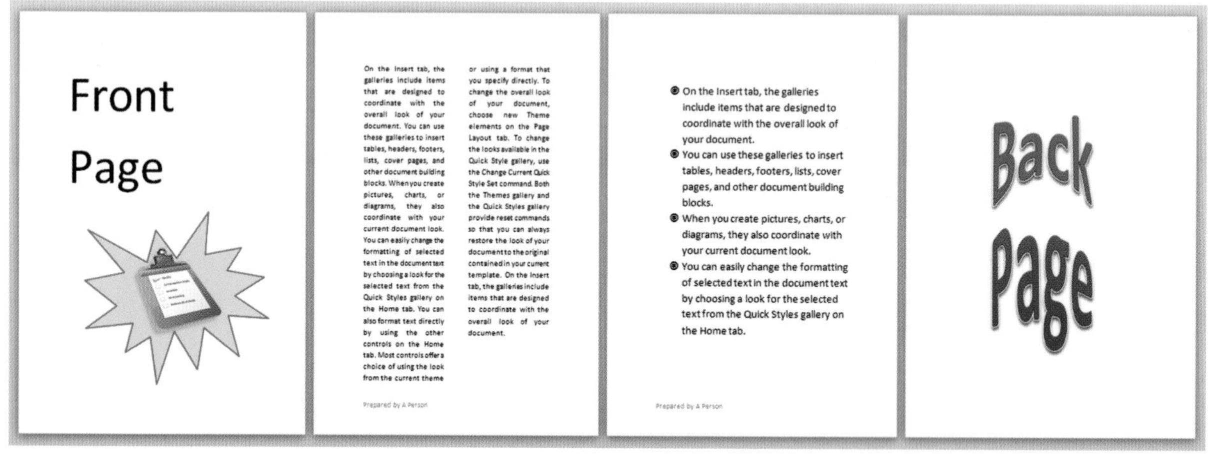

Figure 7.3

Presentations

An Admin Assistant will be required to prepare presentations for other members of staff. Examples of this could include:

- The Sales Manager may need to present up-to-date sales information to Sales Reps.
- The Human Resources department may need to present information to new staff on their Induction Day.
- The Training Manager may need to present information to staff during a Training Event.
- A Manager may need to introduce a speaker at an event organised by the business.

Using presentation software, such PowerPoint® or web-based Prezi, is engaging for the viewer/audience and keeps their attention focused on the speaker/presenter. A variety of equipment is available to make sure that presentations are suitable for audience participation:

- a data projector connected to a computer to display (project) the images on to a large screen
- an interactive whiteboard, again using a data projector but enabling the presenter to interact with the presentation, using special pens and icons which are part of the software program that comes with the whiteboard.

Using presentation software is also a very professional method of communication for the following reasons:

- **transitions** can be set up so that each slide appears in an interesting manner to keep the audience concentrating on the information being presented
- animation of text and graphics can make the presentation very focused
- sound, video clips and hyperlinks to documents or web pages can be incorporated
- timings can be set up so that each slide automatically moves on to the next slide.

Making an effective slideshow presentation using PowerPoint®

- Open a new blank presentation.
- Before proceeding any further it is important that you save the presentation immediately, even though there are no 'slides' except for Title. Save using the filename **Practice Presentation**.
- Choose a Design such as Pushpin; it is a good idea to experiment at this stage and decide on the most appropriate design for the presentation.

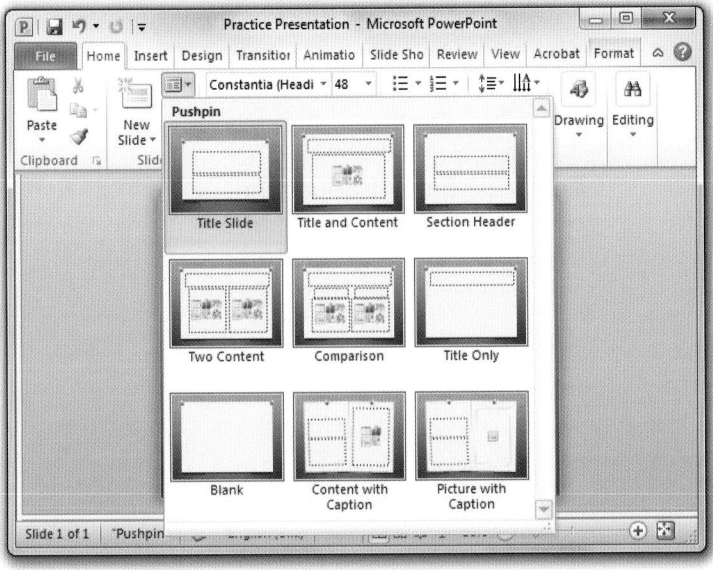

- Once you have decided on the design for the presentation, appropriate slides can be added from the New Slide option.
- The next step is to decide on the fonts, bullets, and so on, for all of the slides; remember: a presentation should have **consistent** fonts for a professional finish.
- Select the Slide Master to format all slides; change the fonts on the Title Master and the Slide Master to a different font, for example Comic Sans.

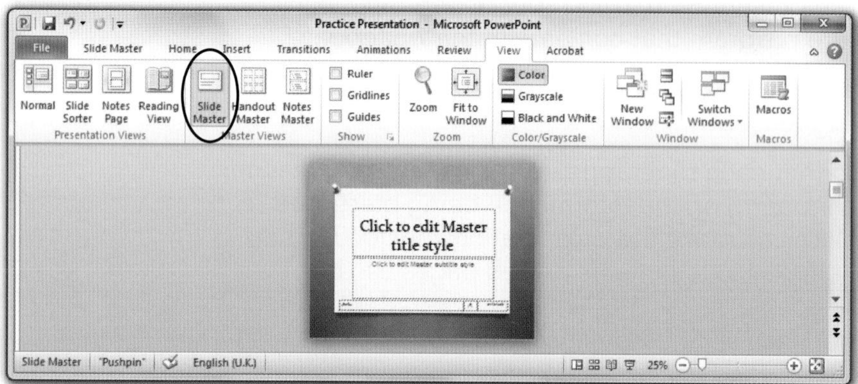

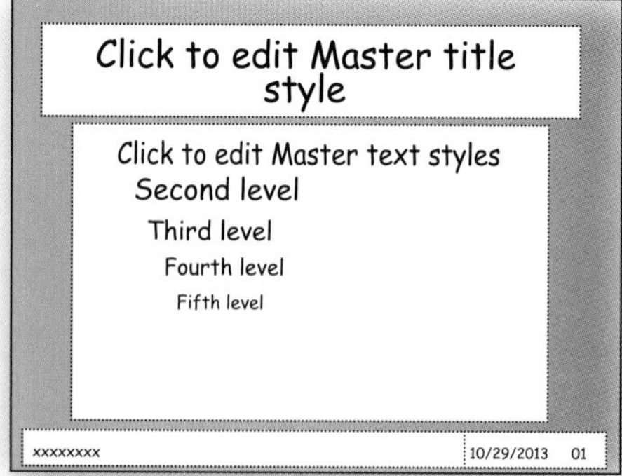

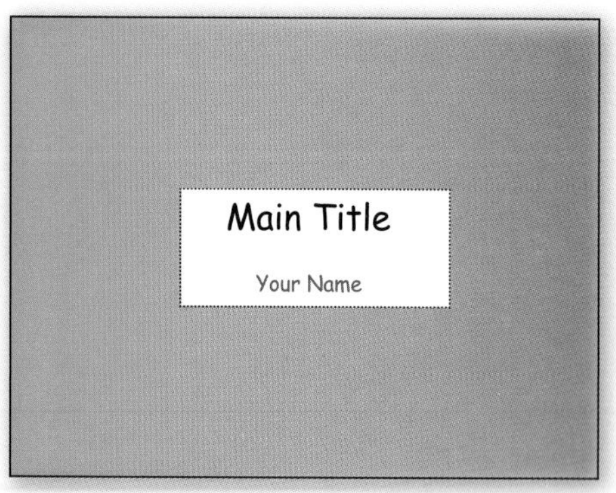

- Title Slide: the two placeholders in this slide are usually used to introduce the topic and either the speaker or more information on the topic.

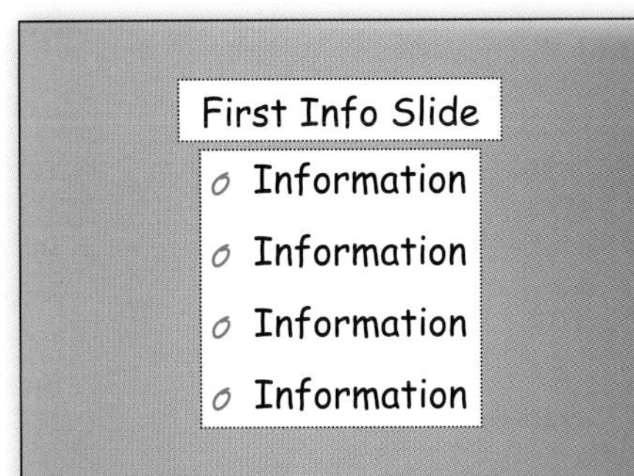

- From the New Slide option select Title and Content. In the top placeholder, a suitable heading can be keyed in and from the choices in the main placeholder, it is easy to insert:
  - **Bulleted Text:** the default
  - **Table:** similar to word processing
  - **Picture from file:** a picture you have previously saved
  - **Chart:** similar to spreadsheet
  - **Clip Art**
  - **Media Clip:** a video clip you have previously saved
  - **SmartArt Graphic:** a DTP feature which allows colourful representations of organisation charts, lists, processes, relationships, and so on.
- From the New Slide option select Two Content Slide; data and picture.

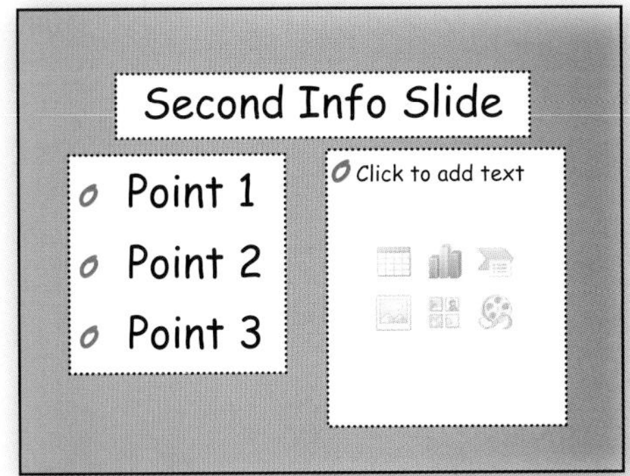

- As for the previous slide, the placeholder's default is bulleted text. Insert a Clip Art picture by simply clicking on the Clip Art icon and selecting an appropriate picture. It is a good idea to use the Search for function for something relevant, for example a clipboard.

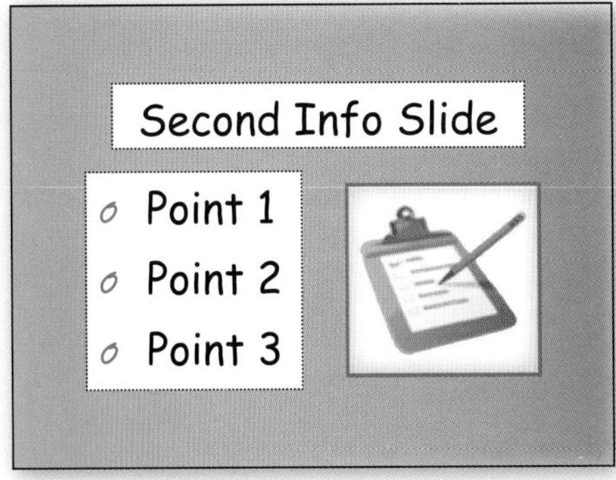

- From the New Slide option select Blank Slide.
- Insert a star shape and key in End of Presentation. Enlarge the shape and the font of the text so that it fills the slide.

The four slides should look something like Figure 7.4.

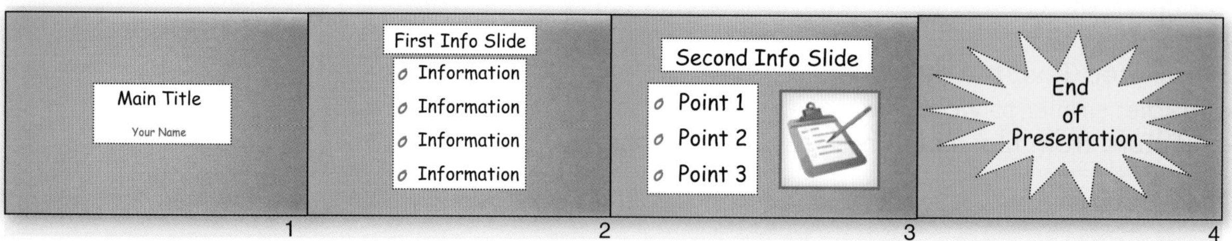

Figure 7.4

Simple presentations can be very effective. However, we can make them even more effective by adding different features.

Transitions

A transition is how each slide appears – automatically or with a click of the mouse.

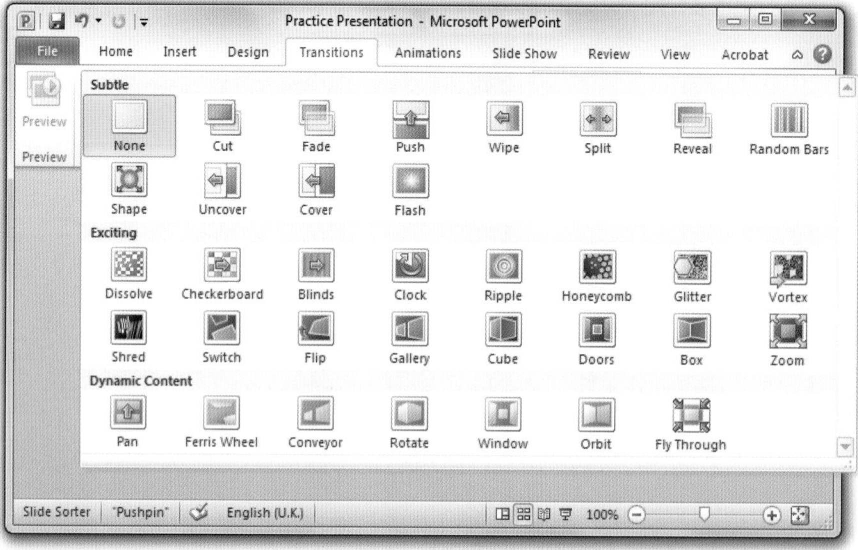

- Select Slide Sorter view.
- Select all slides if you want each slide transition to be the same, or you can apply a different transition to each slide.
- Choose a transition effect from the options available; it should suit the presentation content.
- A small star icon will be visible below each slide to indicate that a transition effect has been applied.

Animations

Animations are how items within each slide appear; automatically, or with a click of the mouse.

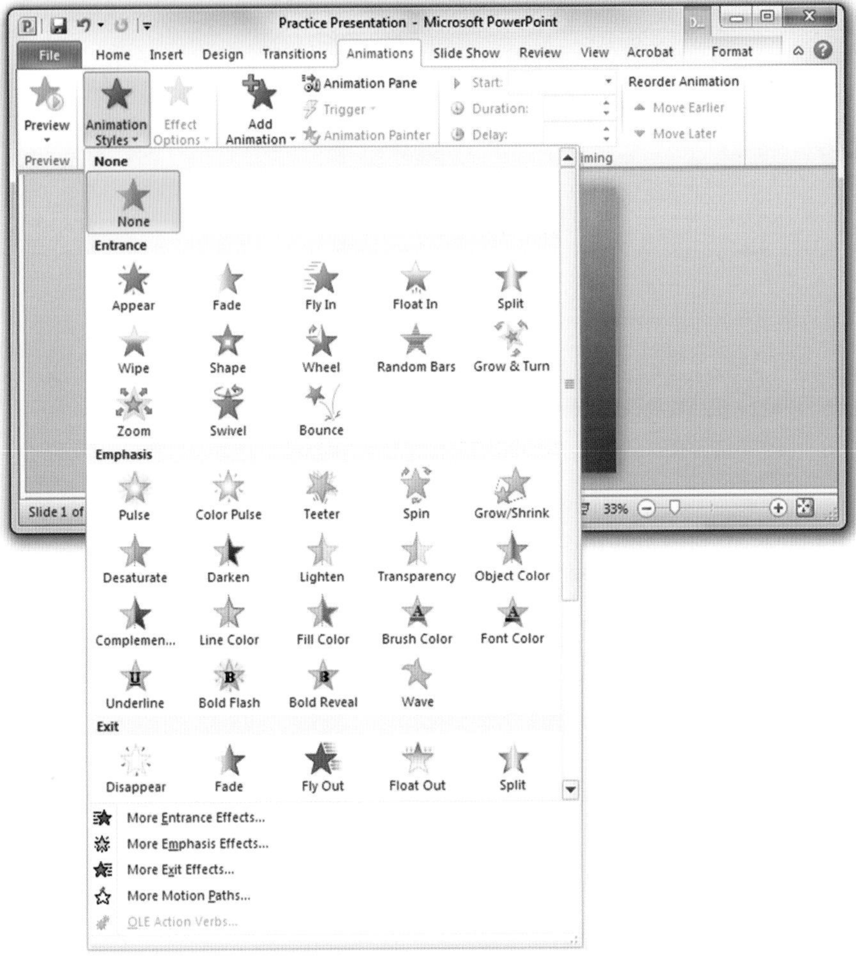

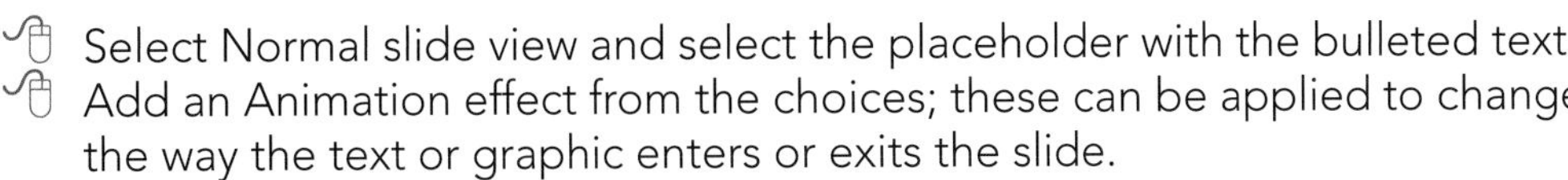

- Select Normal slide view and select the placeholder with the bulleted text.
- Add an Animation effect from the choices; these can be applied to change the way the text or graphic enters or exits the slide.

Sounds

Music and sounds can be added automatically or with a click of the mouse. These can be any sound recording that you have saved previously or taken from the bank of sounds within the software. Once the audio clip has been placed in the slide it can be edited for length and volume, looped, and so on.

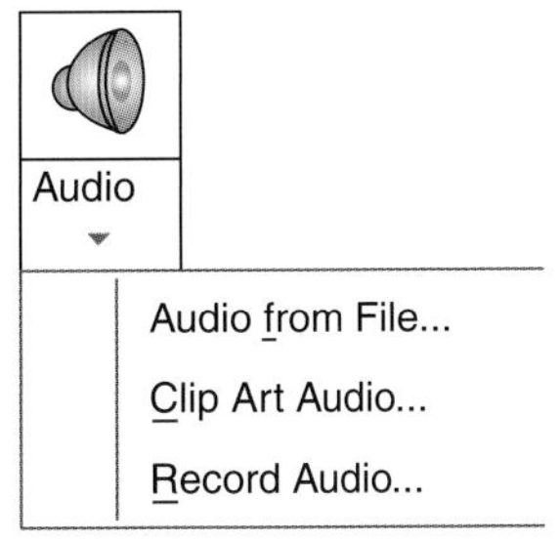

Hyperlinks

Hyperlinks to websites, documents or other slides can be added with a click of the mouse. Select Hyperlink from the Insert ribbon and from the dialog box choose either a web address, document or video or sound file.

Hyperlink

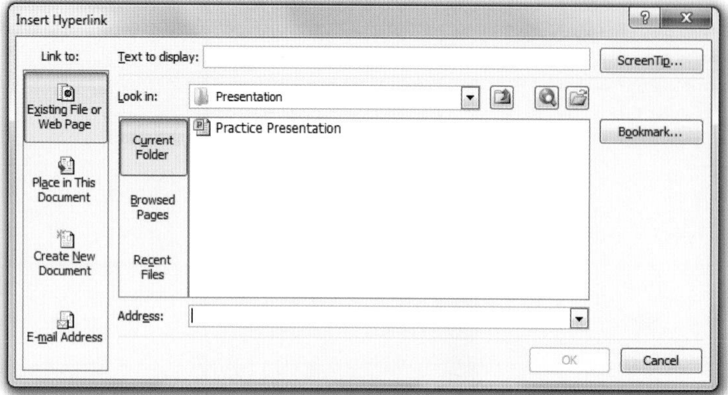

Action buttons

These are icons which link one slide to another and allow the presenter or user to navigate the PowerPoint® presentation by clicking on the action buttons.

- On slide 4, insert an Action button from the options at the bottom of the Shape menu.
- Once the shape is added to the slide, for example the Home icon, the Action Setting menu pops up. Select the slide on which to create the required link; the default is First Slide.

Top tip: Once you decide on a good animation format, it is easy to insert a duplicate slide and simply change the text, and so on. This can save a lot of time.

Printing

Presentations can be printed in slide or handout format; there is also an option for speaker's notes.

Preparing handouts

Firstly, any decision regarding fonts must be made in the Handout Master View.

If the header or footer is long, the text box can be resized in this mode. Any of the headers or footers can be removed, for example the date text box is not always needed and can simply be deleted.

The Handout Master ribbon also allows changes to be made to handout orientation (portrait or landscape), the number of slides per page and items to appear on the handouts, for example the date can be removed from the Handout.

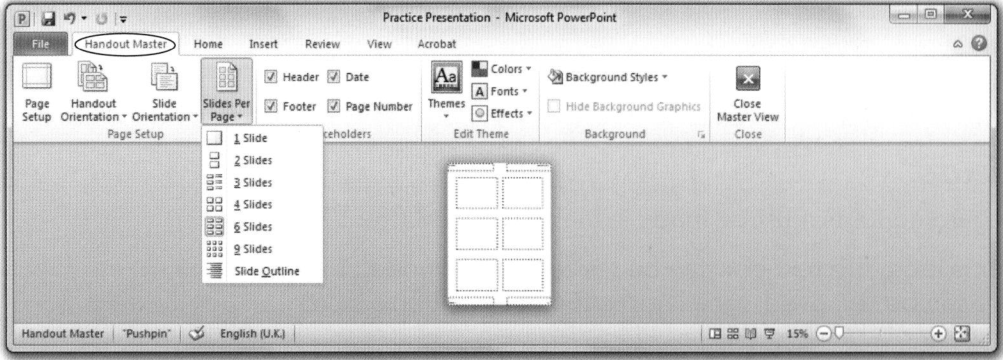

Once the Handout Master has been completed and edited, select the Insert Header and Footer option. The Notes and Handouts tab will pop up, complete with the relevant details.

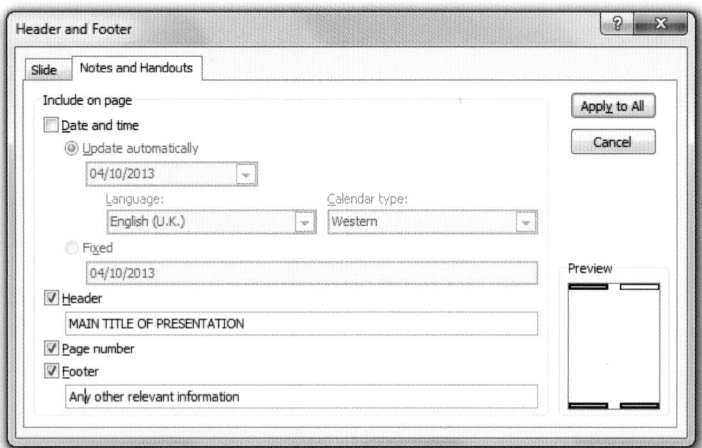

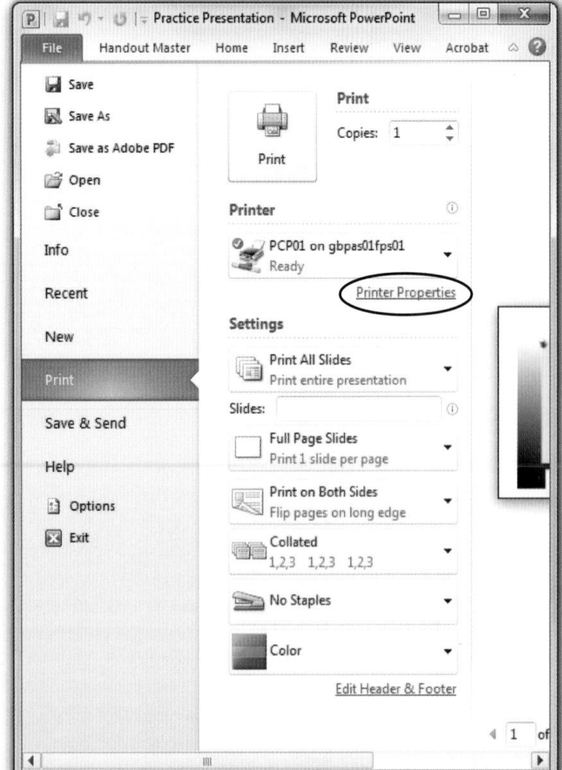

Decisions regarding printing options can be made in the Print dialog box. The options available for back-to-back printing will depend on the type of printer and can be accessed from the Printer Properties.

National 4 & 5 task

Create a presentation to introduce a visiting speaker. Your teacher will decide on the speaker. Only three or four slides are required. Insert a suitable design and graphics, and apply transitions and animations to engage the audience and ensure the information is easy to read. Print the presentation handout on one page or email it to your teacher.

National 4 & 5 task

Complete the following Skills Scan to check your learning. Use the file **Chapter 7 DTP and Presentation Software Skills Scan**. Tick the box that applies to each task.

I can	**easily**	**not sure**	**have difficulty**
Use DTP software to create a poster			
Insert/delete text boxes			
Insert/move shapes			
Insert/format graphics			
Insert headers/footers			
Insert/format borders			
Insert/format shading			
Create and amend presentations – using appropriate software			
Insert/delete/edit text			
Align/format text			
Insert/format graphic			
Use bullets and numbering			
Add/delete slides			
Re-order slides			
Animate text/objects			
Apply slide transitions			
Apply a design			
Print slides and handouts			
National 5 only: Create and amend presentations – using appropriate software			
Insert footer			
Insert action buttons			
Use Slide Master			

Unit 3

Communication in Administration

Chapter 8

Communicating information using technology

By the end of this chapter you will be able to demonstrate an understanding of:

- ✓ the different methods available to communicate information
- ✓ when and why these different methods of communication should be used.

An organisation's ability to communicate information to the right people at the right time is key to any organisation's success. There are now so many ways to communicate with different people, either as groups or individuals, that the difficult task is selecting the best method to use. This is very much dependant on what is being communicated and why it is being communicated.

Organisations communicate with people internally and externally. Communication internally is with staff; however, there are lots of people who organisations communicate with externally:

- customers and potential customers
- suppliers
- other businesses (for example local council, banks).

The use of electronic communication has grown rapidly in recent years and organisations have taken full advantage of these methods, which allow organisations to reach vast numbers of people around the world. This is useful for attracting new customers. It is also relatively inexpensive and some services, such as Facebook and Twitter, can often be free to use.

Email

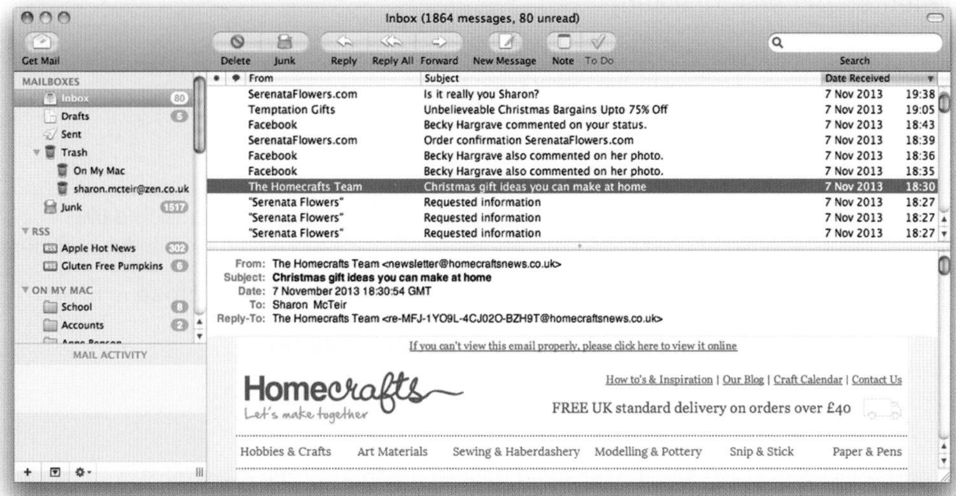

Figure 8.1 Email viewed on a laptop/desktop computer

Emails are commonplace and they can now be sent and received while on the move through smartphones and laptops. The sender needs to know the receiver's email address to send the message. Most organisations have a central address book with contact details of all staff, and then individual staff members can add contacts to their own address book in their email account. An email can be a formal method of communicating and in many cases it is replacing use of the post. As well as a brief message, attachments can also be added.

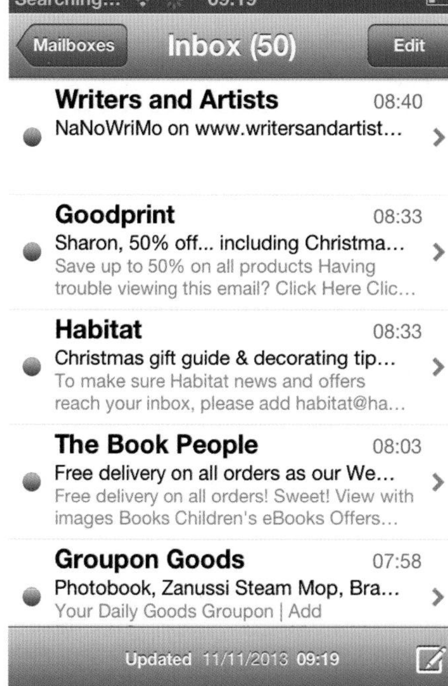

Figure 8.2 Email viewed on a smartphone

There are a number of features of email systems which can help improve communication:

- **Out-of-office reply:** When someone is away for a long period of time, an out-of-office reply can be set up to automatically reply to any email received. The message will advise the sender how long the person will be away and who to contact if the message is urgent or important.
- **Mark urgent:** Messages can be marked as urgent. When the email arrives in the inbox, a mark will appear to show the user that this message is urgent and may encourage them to read this message before others.
- **Read receipt:** Messages can be set up to request that an email be sent back to the sender to let him or her know that their email has been opened.
- **Signature:** Contact details of the sender can be automatically included at the end of the message. This is especially useful when sending an email externally, as often the sender's name, job title, address and telephone number are included.
- **Attachments:** Any file can be attached to an email.

The following are needed when preparing an email:

- email address(es)
- subject: a brief summary of the content of the email
- message text
- any files to be attached to the message.

When composing an email, it is important to think carefully about the content and wording of the message. Although an email is not as formal as a letter, it is still considered a formal method of communicating.

Possible openings	When sending to an individual, start with the person's name. When sending to a group: ■ Dear Colleagues ■ Good afternoon/morning
Main message	There should always be a short message, even if the purpose of the email is to attach a file. Something as simple as: 'Please find attached the presentation for next week.' would be sufficient.
Close	Although it is acceptable to use Yours sincerely/faithfully, this **complimentary close** is more formal and used in letters. Often the following closes are used in email messages: ■ Best regards ■ Regards ■ With regards ■ Kind regards ■ Best wishes The full name of the sender should also be included (unless it is part of the signature).

E-diary

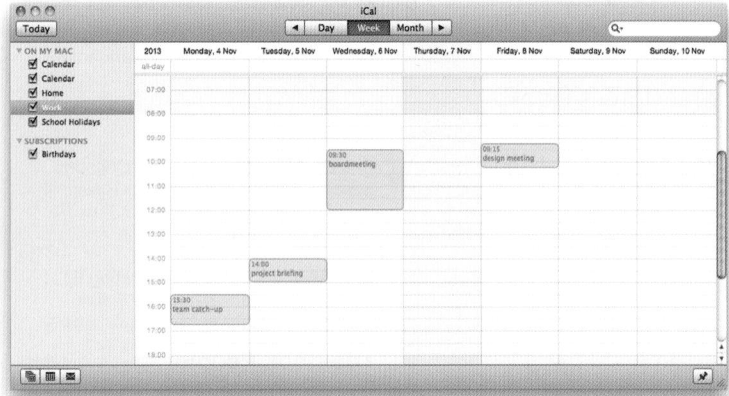

Figure 8.3 E-diary viewed on a laptop/desktop computer

Figure 8.4 E-diary viewed on a smartphone

E-diaries are often used in business to check people's availability and then to invite participants to meetings. The invitation can include details of when, where and how long the meeting will last. Additional information can be added, for example you could attach an agenda.

People will respond to the invitation by accepting, declining or saying they might be able to come along (tentatively accept). This helps the organiser keep track of how many people will be attending.

Appointments can be scheduled in an e-diary so that they repeat on a daily, weekly, monthly or annual basis. This saves having to enter appointments individually.

This method of communication is most often used internally with staff.

Websites

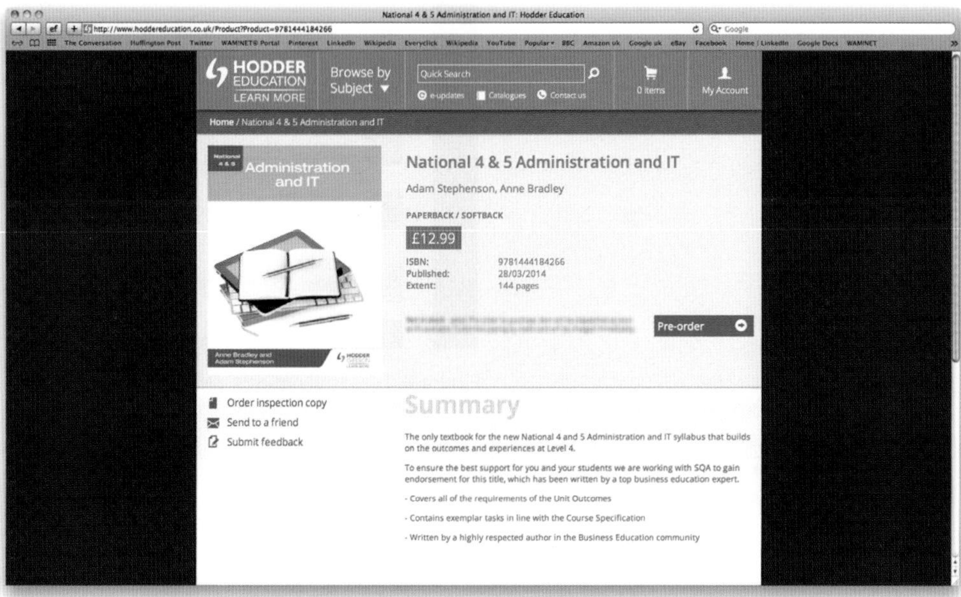

Figure 8.5 A website viewed on a laptop/desktop computer

Organisations often post information on their website. They can include lots of details and even pictures, videos and documents to download. Anyone who has access to the internet can access a website. At the beginning of 2012, 18.8 million UK households had access to broadband and this figure is set to increase (Ofcom 2012, **http://media.ofcom.org.uk/facts/**).

It is important that organisations have a presence on the web. If people are looking for information about a company, its location, opening hours or products, the first port of call is often to search for a company through a search engine. Having this information online and ensuring it is accurate and up to date will encourage customers to use the organisation more. However, there is no method of guaranteeing that the information has been read, as it is dependent on people accessing the website.

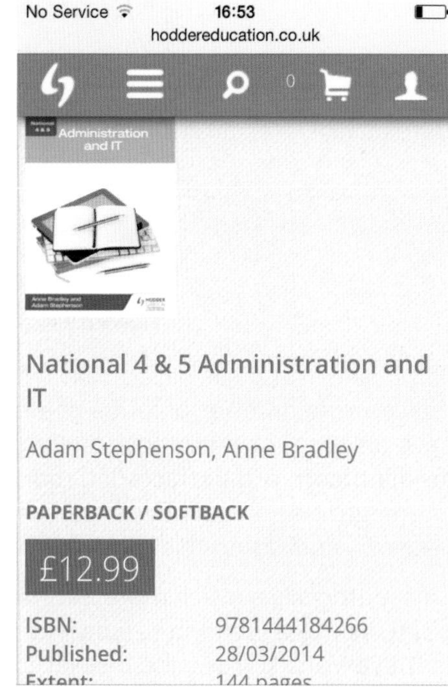

Figure 8.6 A website viewed on a smartphone

Social networks

Figure 8.7 A social network website viewed on a smartphone

Figure 8.8 A social network website viewed on a tablet

Figure 8.9 A social network website viewed on a laptop/desktop computer

Applications such as Facebook, Twitter, LinkedIn, Google+ and YouTube are the latest additions to the growing number of forms of electronic communication available. In the UK, 50 per cent of adults have an account with a social networking site that they access when at home (Ofcom 2012, **http://media.ofcom.org.uk/facts/**). Organisations use these sites to post short pieces of information for interested people to view. Often people have to follow or like an organisation's page on a social network, and doing this gives the company instant access to potential customers.

This method is a much more informal way of communicating. Messages have to be short and to the point, as there is a limit to how much text can be added to each message. There is no guarantee that everyone will see the message; sometimes accounts are not checked regularly, and there are so many posts added to these networks that the message may get lost. Often organisations will post information on more than one social network, as well as on their website.

The information posted on these sites is open to the public. Any posts or replies are visible to anyone, so organisations have to be careful about what they say, and that no personal or confidential information is posted on the site.

Here are some of the things that companies do on their social networking sites:

- alert customers to problems or issues, for example a store is closed or a website or phone line is down
- tell customers about offers or new products/services available
- post videos or photographs
- link to other websites that have more detailed information
- ask customers for questions and feedback.

Text messages

The majority of adults in the UK own a mobile phone (92 per cent of adults in 2012 [Ofcom 2012, **http://media.ofcom.org.uk/facts/**]) and make use of text messaging. The benefit of communicating by text message is that often people have their mobile phone with them at all times, and receiving a text message is less intrusive than a phone call. Messages are less formal, often using text speak, and are short and to the point.

Organisations might send the following information by text:

- update on an order that is due to be delivered
- let customers know about an offer
- remind a customer he or she has an appointment
- ask customers for feedback
- inform customers or suppliers of a problem (for example store closure or service outage).

Sending a text message is a fast and low-cost method of communicating. Messages can be sent to specific customers, so it is more likely that the message will be read than if posting something online; and as people tend to keep their mobiles with them at all times, they may pick up a text faster than an email.

Instant messaging

Many organisations make use of instant messaging (IM) in the workplace. Its use is often encouraged for simple and quick questions to save the time it takes to write out an email or to avoid disturbing someone with a call.

Often organisations have a number of branches or offices across the country and IM applications allow staff to communicate from different locations without the need to travel and avoiding the cost of a call.

Organisations are also able to use this system to broadcast messages to everyone who is logged in. This would be useful if, for example, staff are at work and the network is going to go offline for maintenance; staff can be alerted to this, and the message will not go off the screen until the user has clicked OK.

National 4 task

Please can you email someone in your team to let them know that you have completed work on the presentation for next week's training event? Can you attach the file **Practice Presentation** and ask them to give you any comments they have on it by next week?

Thanks

National 5 task

Can you email the team and remind them about their responsibilities for health and safety at work? Could you mention a few points they need to be aware of – particularly when working on their PCs?
This is really important; we have a health and safety inspection in a few weeks' time and the inspector often asks questions of the staff – can you make sure the team know that this message is very important?

Thanks!

Caroline Marshall, Office Manager

National 4 task

There is a team meeting next Tuesday at 1p.m. in the conference room. Will be finished by 3p.m. Better add this to your diary so you don't forget.

National 5 task

We need to let our customers know that we have changed our opening hours and some of our fees have increased. They should check the website, where they can find out about the changes in the Latest News section.
We don't have our customers' email addresses on record, so can you get this information to them some other way?
Don't print anything out for them though!

Thanks!

Caroline Marshall. Office Manager

National 4 Practice Tasks

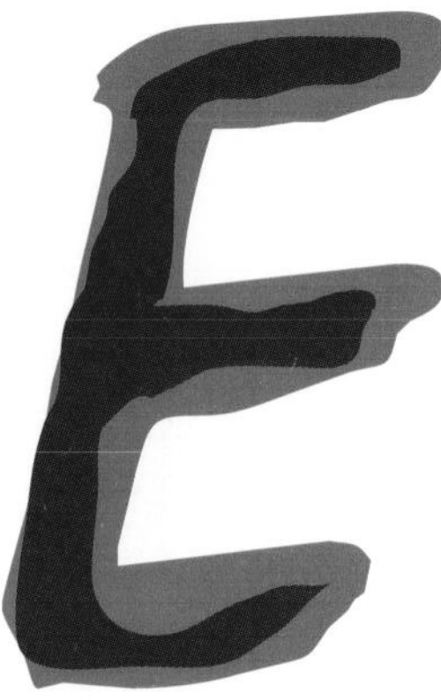

You work as an Administrator for Entertain, a retailer that sells music, films, games and gadgets. You have been asked to support Clare West, Operations Director, who is organising a meeting with staff next Thursday to discuss the new store the company is opening in Aberdeen. Clare has asked you to complete a number of tasks to prepare for the meeting.

Task 1

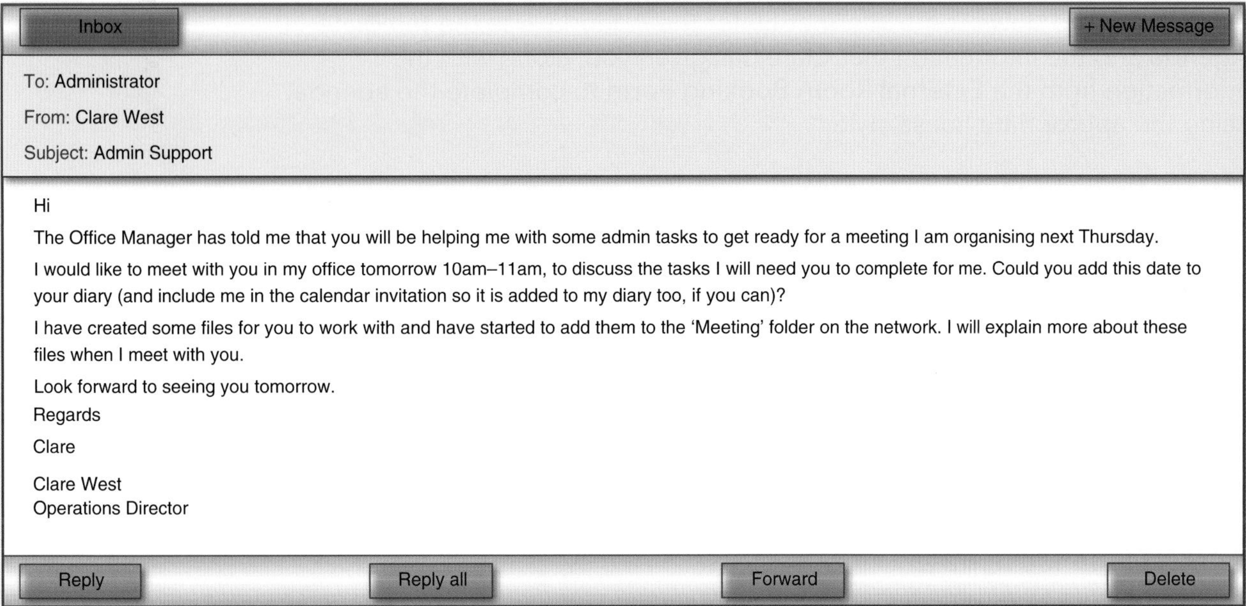
Inbox
+ New Message

To: Administrator
From: Clare West
Subject: Admin Support

Hi

The Office Manager has told me that you will be helping me with some admin tasks to get ready for a meeting I am organising next Thursday.

I would like to meet with you in my office tomorrow 10am–11am, to discuss the tasks I will need you to complete for me. Could you add this date to your diary (and include me in the calendar invitation so it is added to my diary too, if you can)?

I have created some files for you to work with and have started to add them to the 'Meeting' folder on the network. I will explain more about these files when I meet with you.

Look forward to seeing you tomorrow.

Regards

Clare

Clare West
Operations Director

Reply | Reply all | Forward | Delete

Task 2

Use the information below to book a room for the meeting. E-mail a copy of the completed booking form to the address given by your teacher/lecturer.

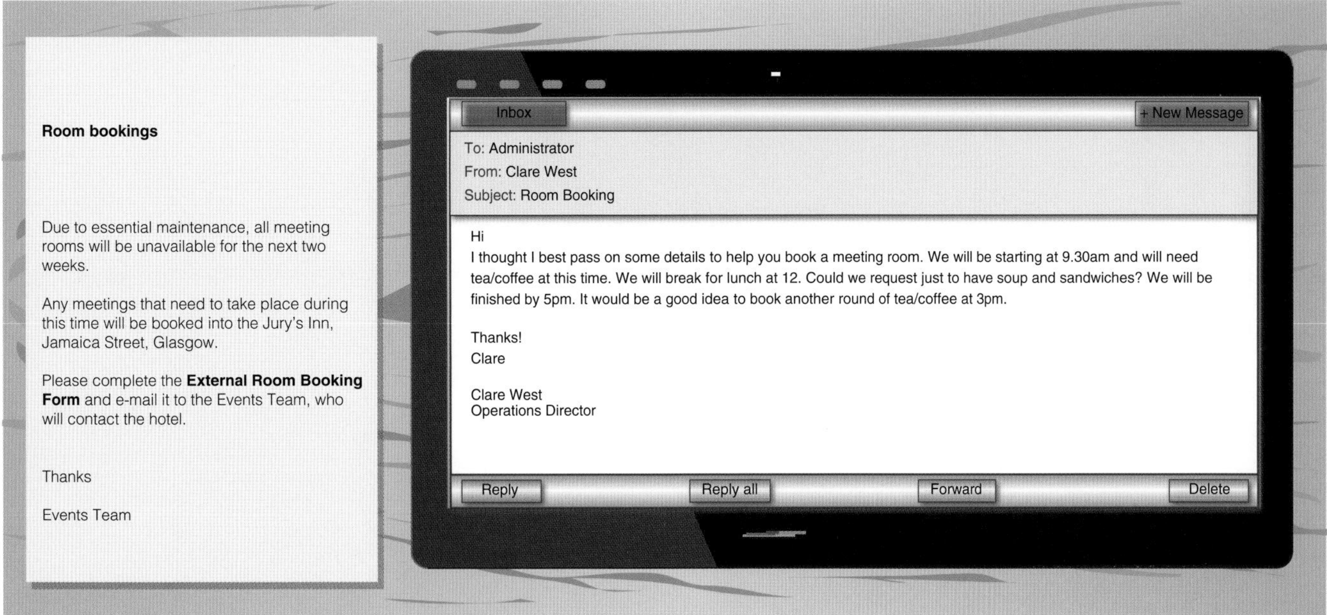
Room bookings

Due to essential maintenance, all meeting rooms will be unavailable for the next two weeks.

Any meetings that need to take place during this time will be booked into the Jury's Inn, Jamaica Street, Glasgow.

Please complete the **External Room Booking Form** and e-mail it to the Events Team, who will contact the hotel.

Thanks

Events Team

Inbox
+ New Message

To: Administrator
From: Clare West
Subject: Room Booking

Hi

I thought I best pass on some details to help you book a meeting room. We will be starting at 9.30am and will need tea/coffee at this time. We will break for lunch at 12. Could we request just to have soup and sandwiches? We will be finished by 5pm. It would be a good idea to book another round of tea/coffee at 3pm.

Thanks!
Clare

Clare West
Operations Director

Reply | Reply all | Forward | Delete

Task 3

Clare has noted down some information for the Agenda. Use the template **Agenda** and the information that Clare has given you, along with the information from the **External Room Booking Form** to complete the agenda, using the appropriate house style.

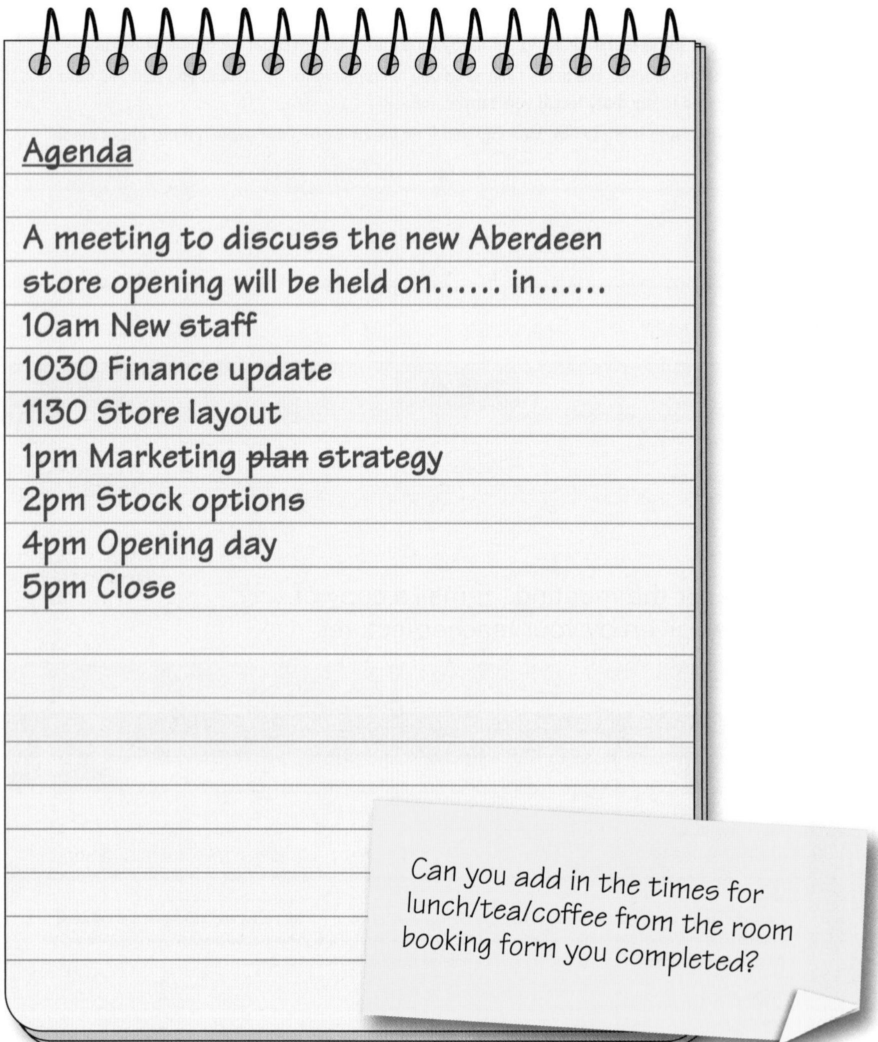

Agenda
A meeting to discuss the new Aberdeen
store opening will be held on...... in......
10am New staff
1030 Finance update
1130 Store layout
1pm Marketing ~~plan~~ strategy
2pm Stock options
4pm Opening day
5pm Close
Can you add in the times for lunch/tea/coffee from the room booking form you completed?

Task 4

You have received the following messages about your room booking.

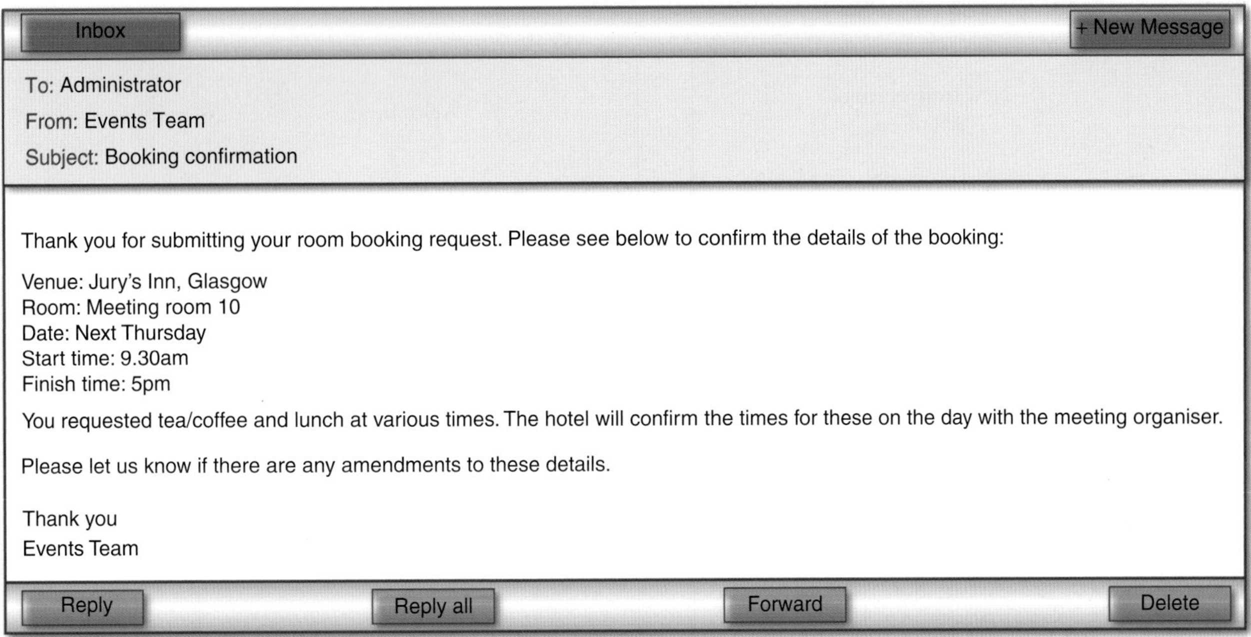

Inbox + New Message

To: Administrator
From: Events Team
Subject: Booking confirmation

Thank you for submitting your room booking request. Please see below to confirm the details of the booking:

Venue: Jury's Inn, Glasgow
Room: Meeting room 10
Date: Next Thursday
Start time: 9.30am
Finish time: 5pm

You requested tea/coffee and lunch at various times. The hotel will confirm the times for these on the day with the meeting organiser.

Please let us know if there are any amendments to these details.

Thank you
Events Team

Reply Reply all Forward Delete

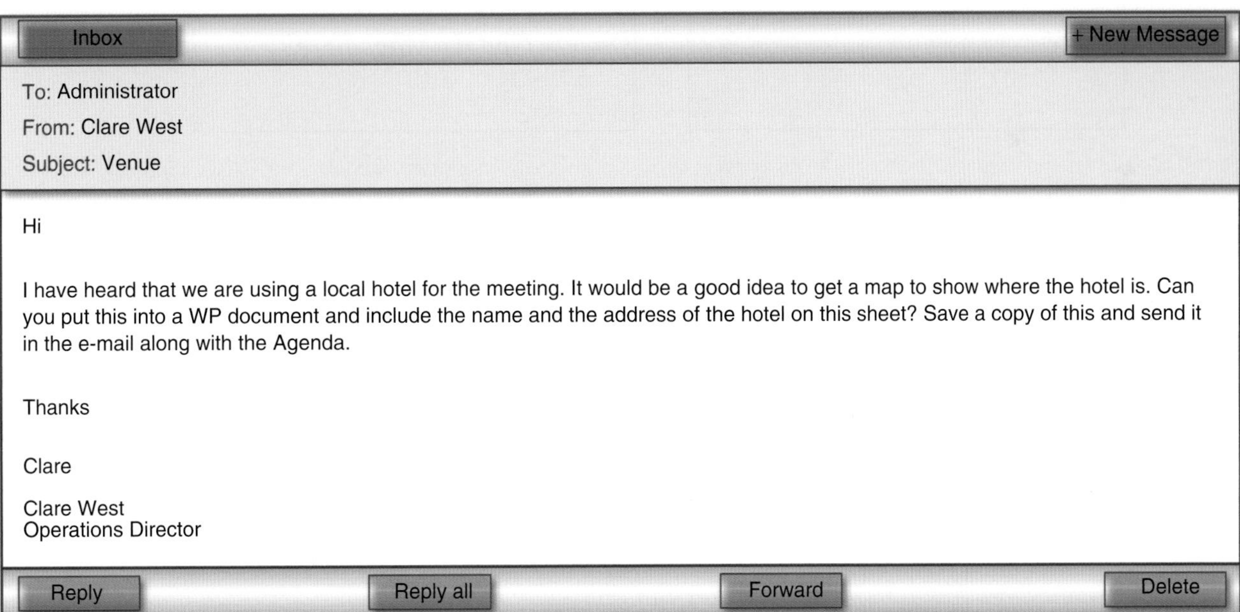

Inbox + New Message

To: Administrator
From: Clare West
Subject: Venue

Hi

I have heard that we are using a local hotel for the meeting. It would be a good idea to get a map to show where the hotel is. Can you put this into a WP document and include the name and the address of the hotel on this sheet? Save a copy of this and send it in the e-mail along with the Agenda.

Thanks

Clare

Clare West
Operations Director

Reply Reply all Forward Delete

Task 5

Clare will be displaying a presentation during the meeting. Use the information below to update the file **Meeting presentation**.

New store opening
Aberdeen

Insert the company logo from file ***Logo*** *here*

Welcome

Insert the timings from the agenda you created into this slide

New staff

- Recruitment completed
- Training starts next week
- New uniform launched with this store
- Staff contracts are being finalised

Find and insert a suitable graphic from the internet here

Store location

Insert a map of Aberdeen city centre from Google Maps here

Finance update

Insert the list sent from the Finance Director from file ***Update*** *here*

Marketing strategy

Insert the list sent from the Marketing Director from file Update here

Opening day

- *Two months to go*
- *First 20 customers will receive £100 (gift vouchers) and 10% (discount)*
- *Buffet and drinks for customers throughout the day*
- *First week, all customers receive 10% off purchases*
- *Information being sent to all local press*

Add a design template to the presentation.
Add an interesting transition effect – the same one for the whole presentation.
Print the slides, three per page, with space for me to make notes and e-mail me a copy.
Clare

Task 6

The events team has started to record the costs of the meeting in order to create the budget. The budget must be sent to the Finance department before the meeting. Complete the spreadsheet file **Venue costing** using the information below and the information from the **External Room Booking Form** you completed.

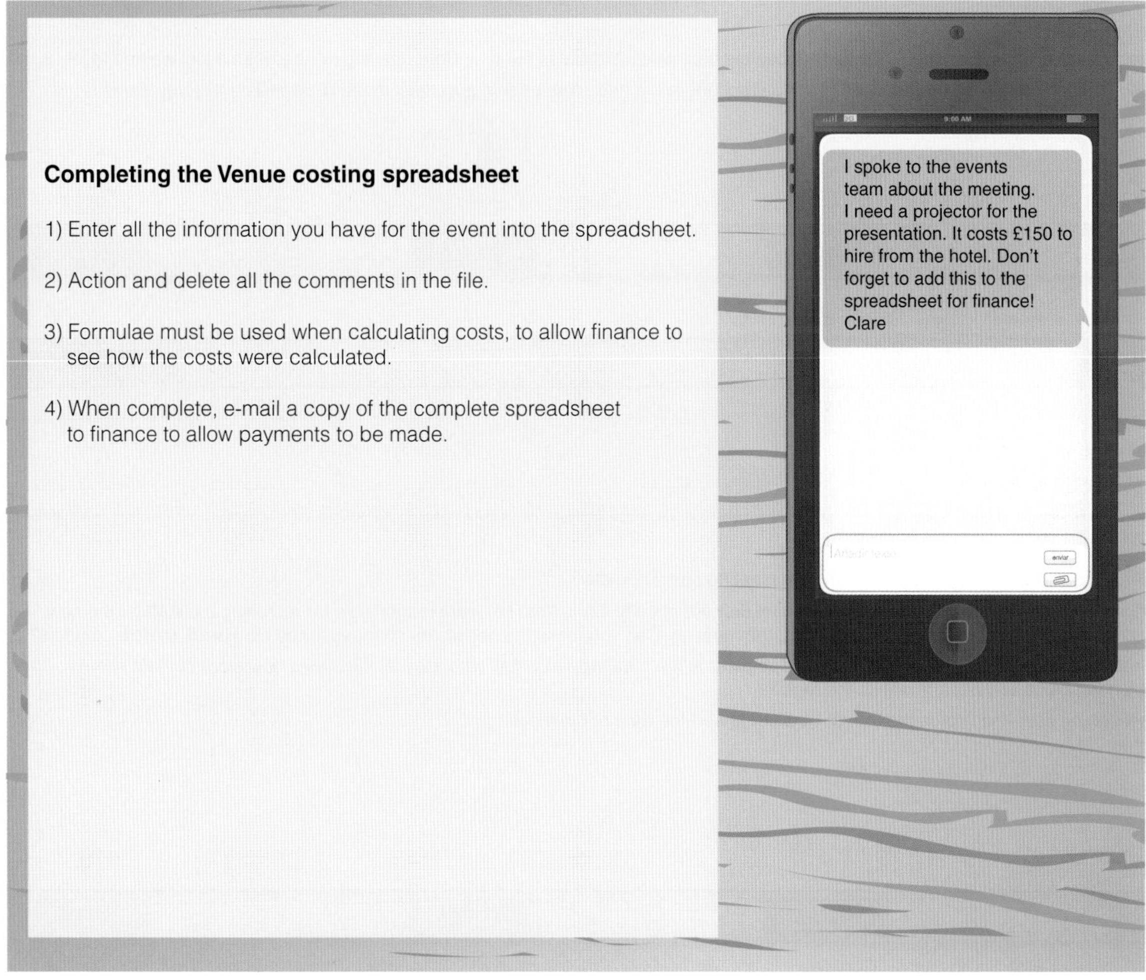

Completing the Venue costing spreadsheet
1) Enter all the information you have for the event into the spreadsheet.
2) Action and delete all the comments in the file.
3) Formulae must be used when calculating costs, to allow finance to see how the costs were calculated.
4) When complete, e-mail a copy of the complete spreadsheet to finance to allow payments to be made.
I spoke to the events team about the meeting. I need a projector for the presentation. It costs £150 to hire from the hotel. Don't forget to add this to the spreadsheet for finance! Clare

Task 7

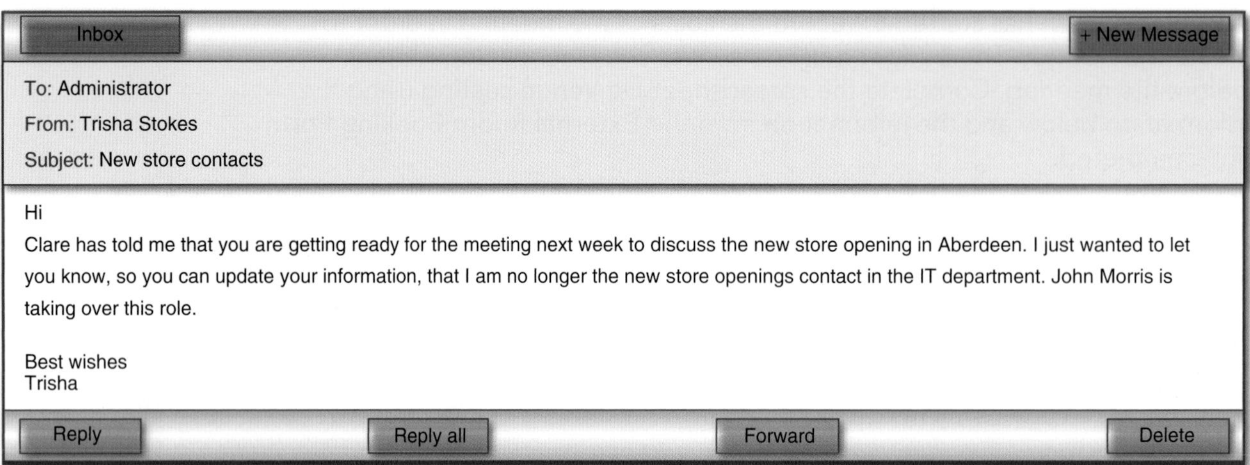

To: Administrator
From: Trisha Stokes
Subject: New store contacts

Hi

Clare has told me that you are getting ready for the meeting next week to discuss the new store opening in Aberdeen. I just wanted to let you know, so you can update your information, that I am no longer the new store openings contact in the IT department. John Morris is taking over this role.

Best wishes
Trisha

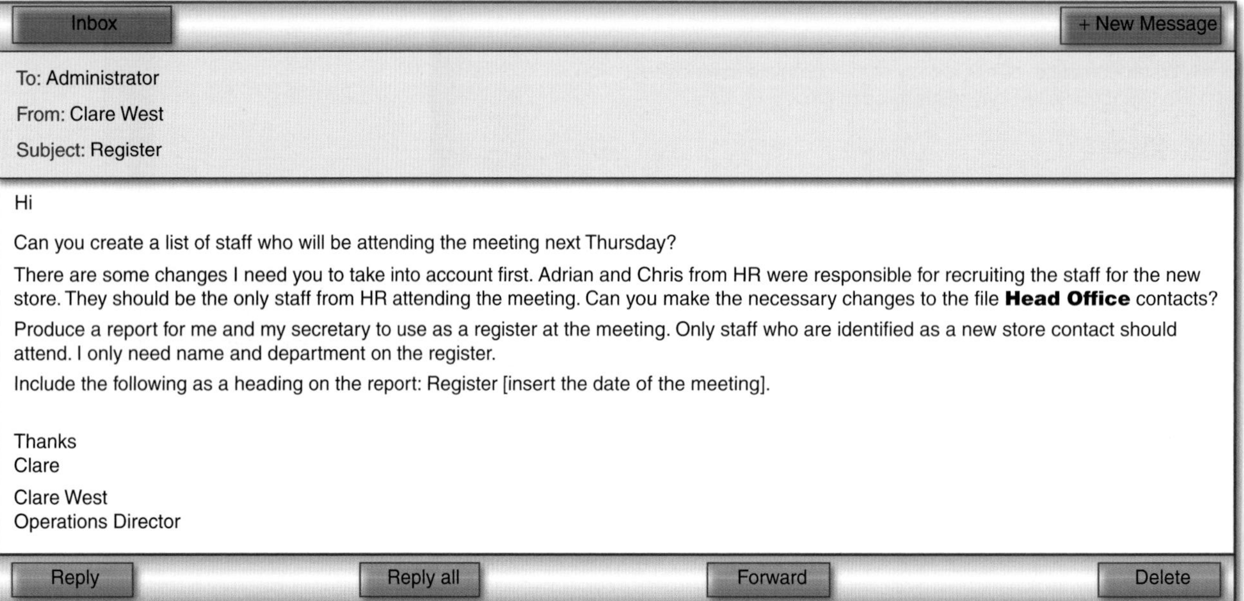

To: Administrator
From: Clare West
Subject: Register

Hi

Can you create a list of staff who will be attending the meeting next Thursday?

There are some changes I need you to take into account first. Adrian and Chris from HR were responsible for recruiting the staff for the new store. They should be the only staff from HR attending the meeting. Can you make the necessary changes to the file **Head Office** contacts?

Produce a report for me and my secretary to use as a register at the meeting. Only staff who are identified as a new store contact should attend. I only need name and department on the register.

Include the following as a heading on the report: Register [insert the date of the meeting].

Thanks
Clare

Clare West
Operations Director

Task 8

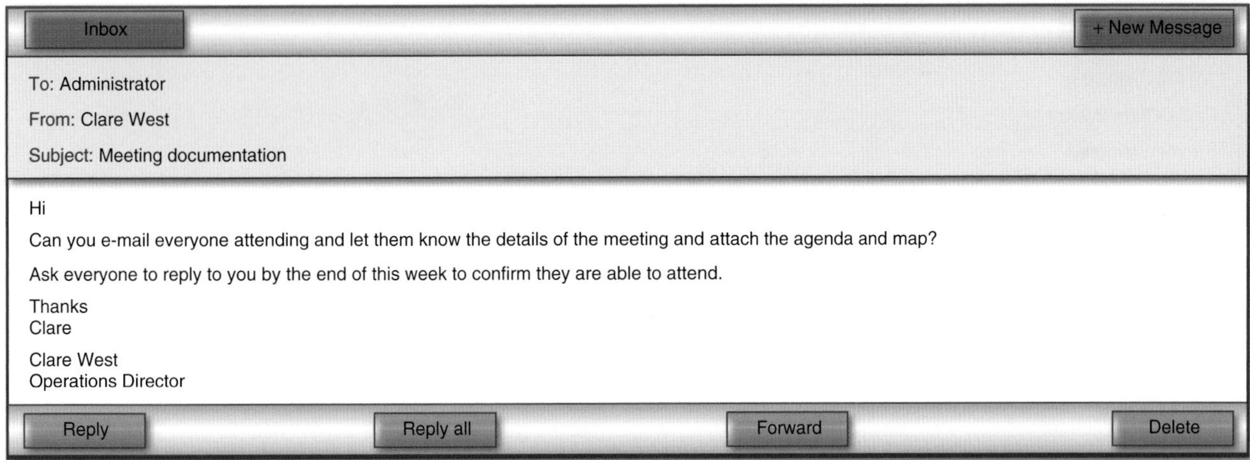
Inbox
+ New Message
To: Administrator
From: Clare West
Subject: Meeting documentation
Hi
Can you e-mail everyone attending and let them know the details of the meeting and attach the agenda and map?
Ask everyone to reply to you by the end of this week to confirm they are able to attend.
Thanks
Clare
Clare West
Operations Director
Reply
Reply all
Forward
Delete

Task 9

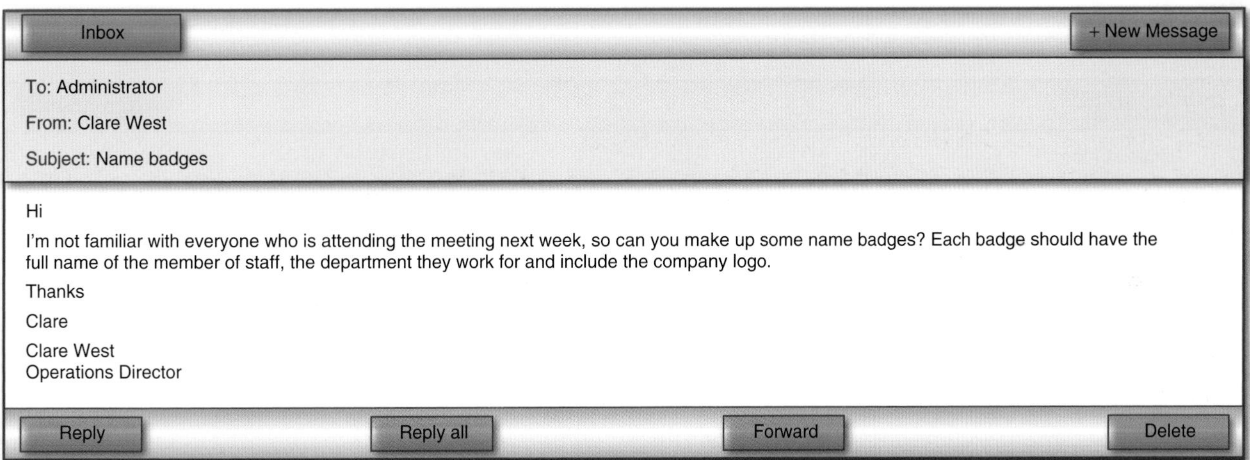
Inbox
+ New Message
To: Administrator
From: Clare West
Subject: Name badges
Hi
I'm not familiar with everyone who is attending the meeting next week, so can you make up some name badges? Each badge should have the full name of the member of staff, the department they work for and include the company logo.
Thanks
Clare
Clare West
Operations Director
Reply
Reply all
Forward
Delete

Task 10

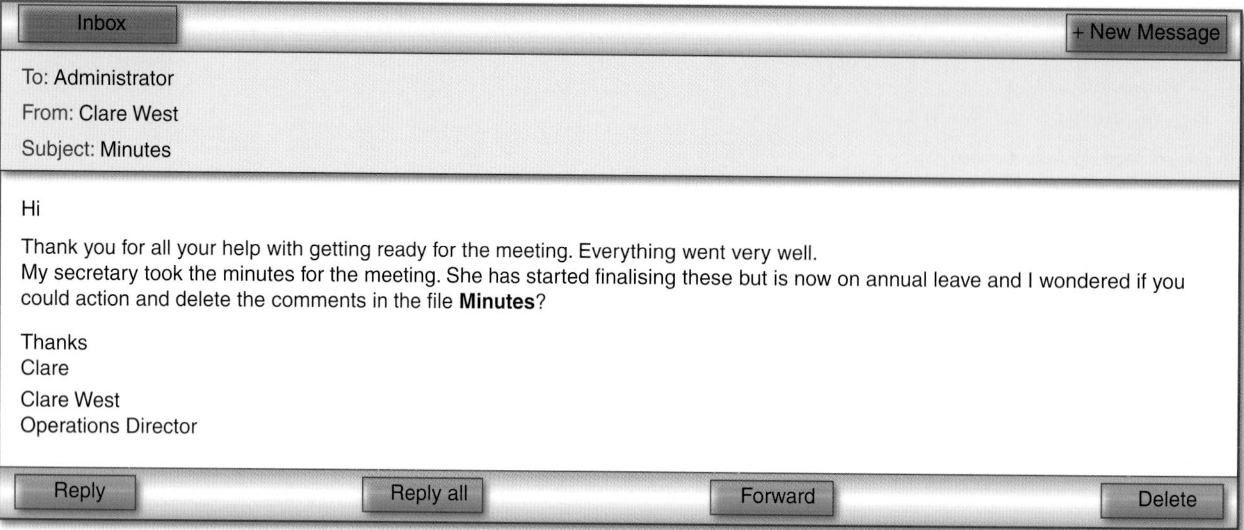

Inbox
+ New Message
To: Administrator
From: Clare West
Subject: Minutes
Hi
Thank you for all your help with getting ready for the meeting. Everything went very well.
My secretary took the minutes for the meeting. She has started finalising these but is now on annual leave and I wondered if you could action and delete the comments in the file **Minutes**?
Thanks
Clare
Clare West
Operations Director
Reply
Reply all
Forward
Delete

Task 11

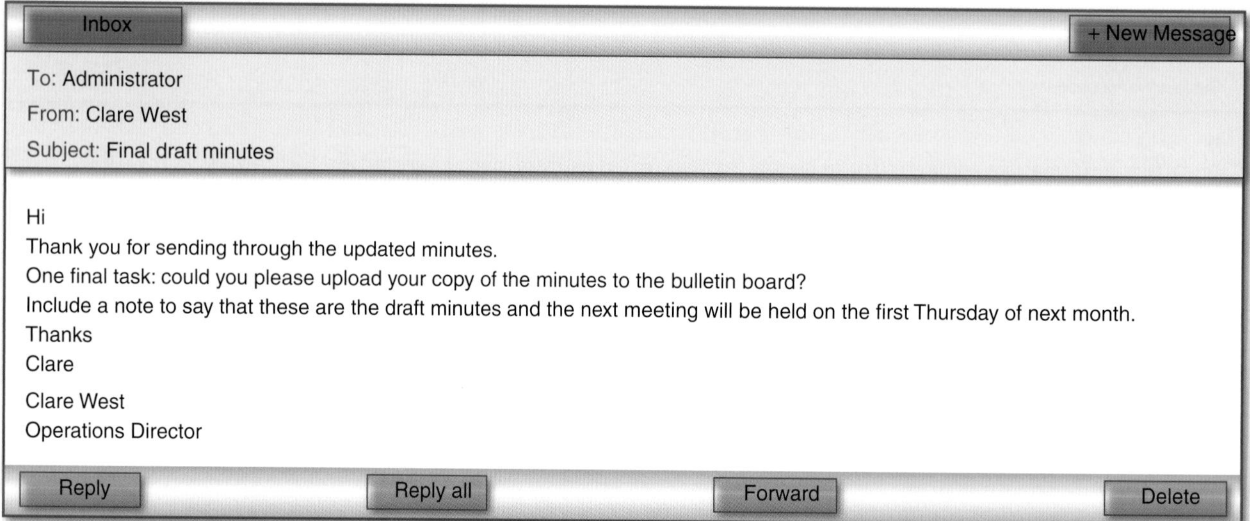

Inbox
+ New Message
To: Administrator
From: Clare West
Subject: Final draft minutes
Hi
Thank you for sending through the updated minutes.
One final task: could you please upload your copy of the minutes to the bulletin board?
Include a note to say that these are the draft minutes and the next meeting will be held on the first Thursday of next month.
Thanks
Clare
Clare West
Operations Director
Reply
Reply all
Forward
Delete

National 5 Practice Tasks

You work as an Administrator for Entertain, a retailer that sells music, films, games and gadgets. You have been asked to support James Bradley, Area Manager – Scotland, as he prepares for the opening of a new store in Aberdeen. James has asked you to complete a number of tasks to prepare for the opening of the new store.

Task 1

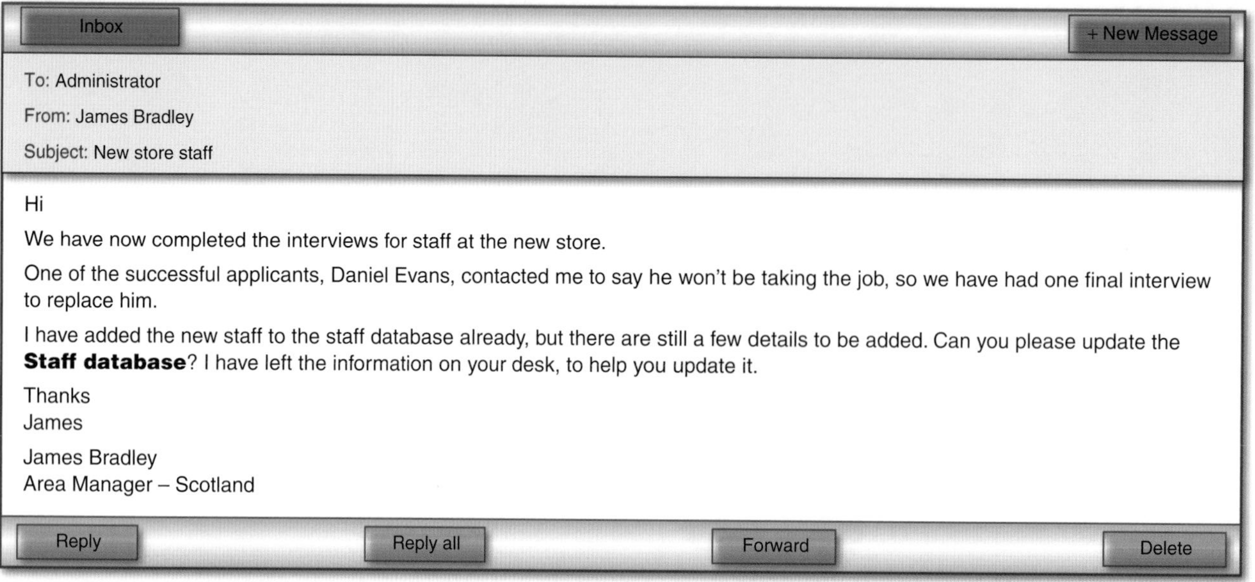

Inbox | + New Message

To: Administrator

From: James Bradley

Subject: New store staff

Hi

We have now completed the interviews for staff at the new store.

One of the successful applicants, Daniel Evans, contacted me to say he won't be taking the job, so we have had one final interview to replace him.

I have added the new staff to the staff database already, but there are still a few details to be added. Can you please update the **Staff database**? I have left the information on your desk, to help you update it.

Thanks
James

James Bradley
Area Manager – Scotland

Reply | Reply all | Forward | Delete

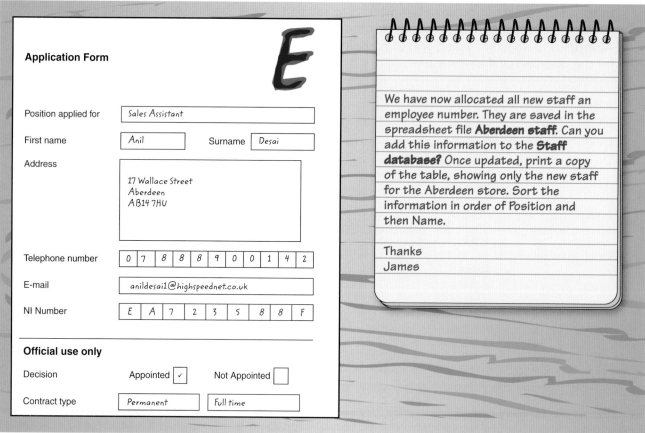

Application Form E

Position applied for	Sales Assistant
First name	Anil
Surname	Desai
Address	17 Wallace Street Aberdeen AB14 7HU
Telephone number	0 7 8 8 8 9 0 0 1 4 2
E-mail	anildesai1@highspeednet.co.uk
NI Number	E A 7 2 3 5 8 8 F

Official use only

Decision	Appointed ✓ Not Appointed ☐
Contract type	Permanent / Full time

We have now allocated all new staff an employee number. They are saved in the spreadsheet file **Aberdeen staff**. Can you add this information to the **Staff database?** Once updated, print a copy of the table, showing only the new staff for the Aberdeen store. Sort the information in order of Position and then Name.

Thanks
James

Task 2

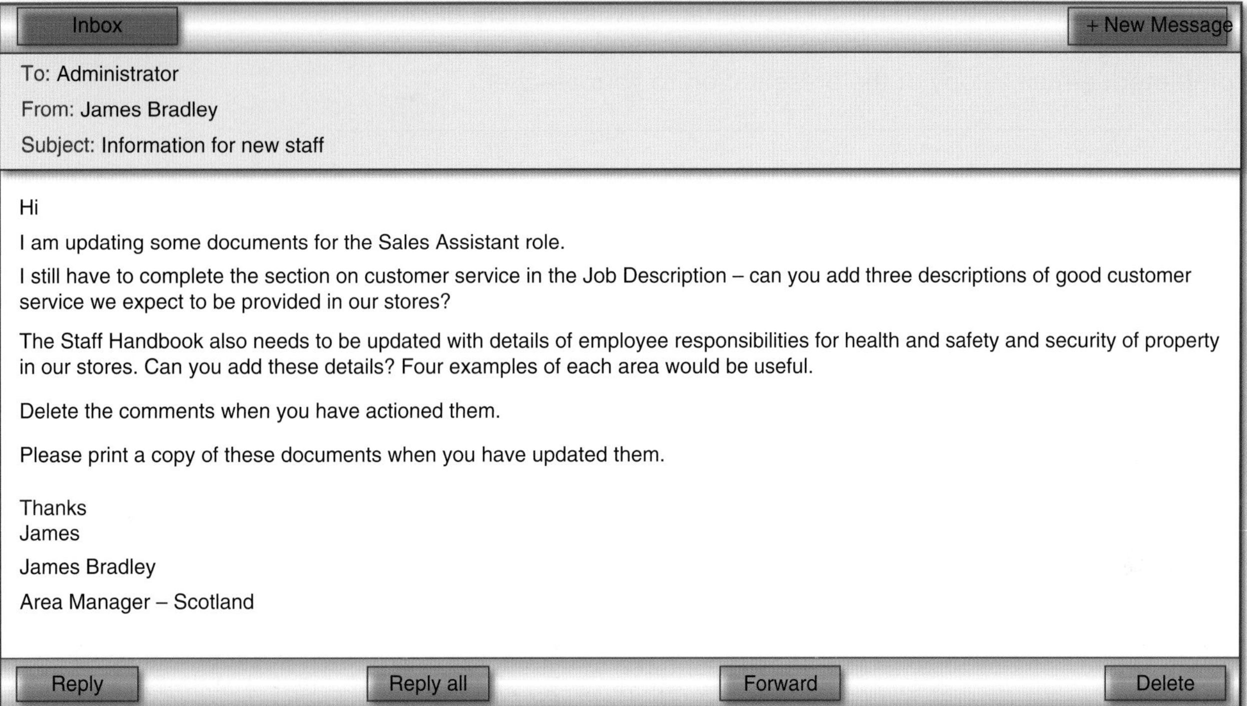
Inbox
+ New Message

To: Administrator
From: James Bradley
Subject: Information for new staff

Hi

I am updating some documents for the Sales Assistant role.

I still have to complete the section on customer service in the Job Description – can you add three descriptions of good customer service we expect to be provided in our stores?

The Staff Handbook also needs to be updated with details of employee responsibilities for health and safety and security of property in our stores. Can you add these details? Four examples of each area would be useful.

Delete the comments when you have actioned them.

Please print a copy of these documents when you have updated them.

Thanks
James

James Bradley

Area Manager – Scotland

Reply
Reply all
Forward
Delete

Task 3

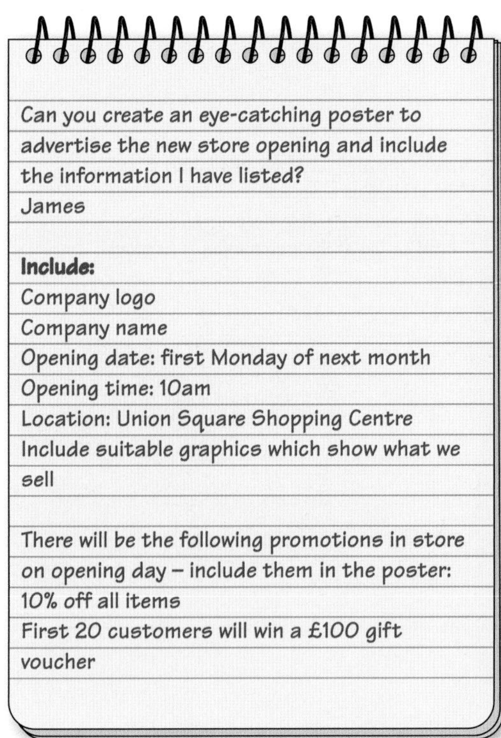
Can you create an eye-catching poster to advertise the new store opening and include the information I have listed?
James

Include:
Company logo
Company name
Opening date: first Monday of next month
Opening time: 10am
Location: Union Square Shopping Centre
Include suitable graphics which show what we sell

There will be the following promotions in store on opening day – include them in the poster:
10% off all items
First 20 customers will win a £100 gift voucher

Task 4

James has asked you to update the presentation which will be displayed in store during the opening day. He has supplied some notes for you. Once completed, e-mail a copy of the presentation to your teacher.

Insert the logo and company name here

Welcome to your new
Aberdeen Store!

Meet your Store Manager
John Duffy

insert the photo of John Duffy

Insert the offers that will be in store for opening day - details in the poster. One offer per slide and include a suitable picture

Store opening hours

Make this the 2nd slide

	Opens	*Closes*
Monday	*9 am*	*6 pm*
Tuesday	*9 am*	*6 pm*
Wednesday	*9 am*	*6 pm*
Thursday	*9 am*	*10 pm*
Friday	*9 am*	*6 pm*
Saturday	*9 am*	*7 pm*
Sunday	*10 am*	*5 pm*

** Insert the company logo on all slides except the first one.*
** Apply a suitable slide design to all slides.*
** Print a copy of the presentation in handout view.*

Task 5

James has started a letter to be sent to the Sales Assistants at the new Aberdeen store.

Complete the letter and add the following after the first paragraph in his draft.

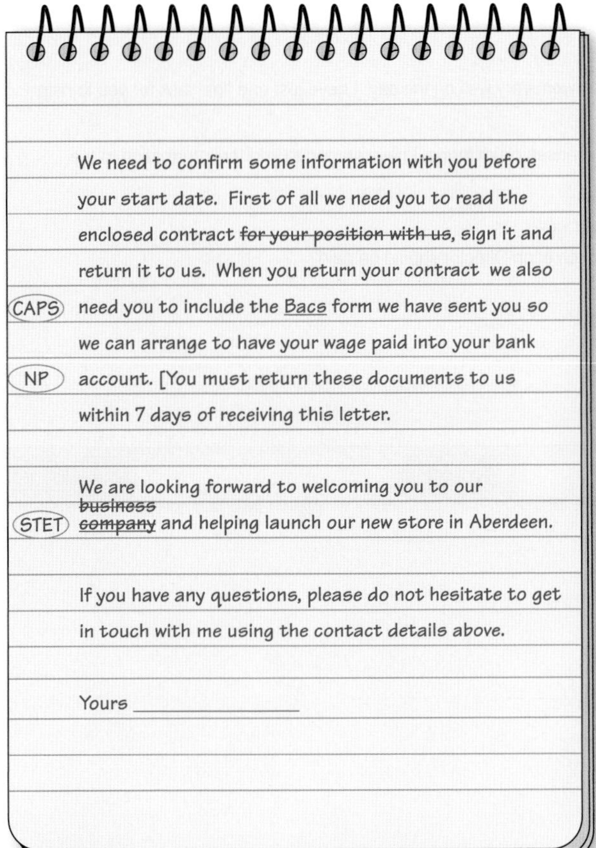

We need to confirm some information with you before your start date. First of all we need you to read the enclosed contract ~~for your position with us~~, sign it and return it to us. When you return your contract we also

(CAPS) need you to include the Bacs form we have sent you so we can arrange to have your wage paid into your bank

(NP) account. [You must return these documents to us within 7 days of receiving this letter.

We are looking forward to welcoming you to our

~~business~~

(STET) ~~company~~ and helping launch our new store in Aberdeen.

If you have any questions, please do not hesitate to get in touch with me using the contact details above.

Yours ______________

Add to your e-diary, 7 days from today, an entry to remind you that contracts must be received from new Aberdeen staff. Set as an all-day event. Print me a copy in day view.

Task 6

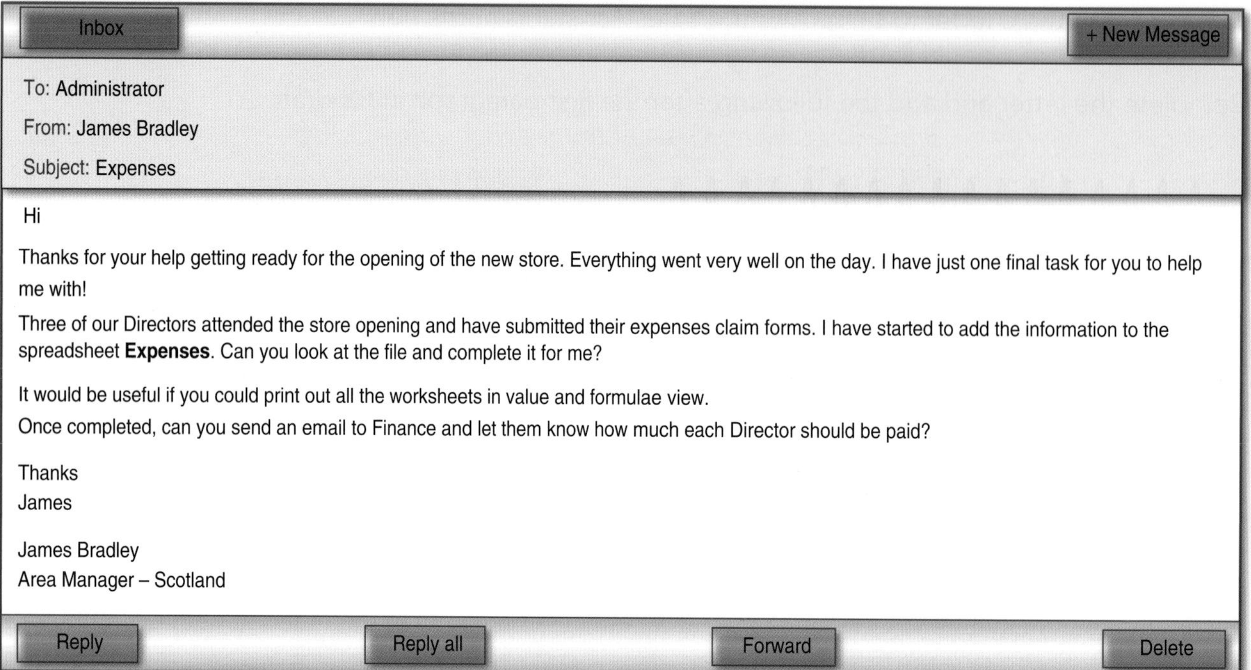
Inbox
+ New Message

To: Administrator
From: James Bradley
Subject: Expenses

Hi

Thanks for your help getting ready for the opening of the new store. Everything went very well on the day. I have just one final task for you to help me with!

Three of our Directors attended the store opening and have submitted their expenses claim forms. I have started to add the information to the spreadsheet **Expenses**. Can you look at the file and complete it for me?

It would be useful if you could print out all the worksheets in value and formulae view.
Once completed, can you send an email to Finance and let them know how much each Director should be paid?

Thanks
James

James Bradley
Area Manager – Scotland

Reply Reply all Forward Delete

Appendix

Manuscript correction signs

Almost all manuscript correction signs (or proofreading symbols) follow the same pattern. There is a mark in the margin (left or right) along with specific information about the change to be made. A mark will also be made in the text where the change is to be made.

Sign in Margin[1]	Example of what is shown on the document	What it means
UC or CAPS	an aquathon	Change the underlined letter **a** to a capital letter (upper case). … an Aquathon
lc	Yours Faithfully	Change the underlined letter **F** to a small letter (lower case). Yours faithfully
u/s	Computers	Apply underline to Computers – the underlined word. Computers
bold	Select the control key.	Change the underlined word control to bold format. Select the **control** key.
italics	as appropriate	Change the underlined words as appropriate to italic format. … *as appropriate* ….
	We c an help	Remove the space between the word to read: We can help
N.P.	competition. [The race results	Create a new paragraph at the place indicated. (Hint – press enter twice.) ………………………….. competition. The race results …..
run on	for your final afternoon. Please advise	Join two paragraphs into one. For your final afternoon. Please advise
	as in the previous years.	Delete the scored out word the as indicated. … as in previous years.
constantly	are trying to improve	Insert the word constantly at the place indicated. … are constantly trying to improve
TRS	commitment and efforts.	Change the order of the words as indicated (horizontally). … efforts and commitment.

[1] A correction made in the document usually has a corresponding mark in the margin, otherwise it could be easily missed when corrections are being made.

Sign in Margin	Example of what is shown on the document	What it means
trs	English Administration	Change the order of the words as indicated (vertically). Administration English
	Change margins to 2·54cm (1 inch)	Follow the instructions[2] within the circle – do not key-in the words in the circle. Use Page Setup to change margins.
stet	we are ~~happy~~ ~~delighted~~	Keep the cancelled word delighted indicated by the dotted line[3]– … we are delighted ….
In full	bed & breakfast	Change the underlined abbreviation & to the full meaning … bed and breakfast
interruption	Unclear or unusual word is normally underlined	This is used when a word is unclear/unusual and it is most commonly used to confirm the spelling … interruption.

[2] Where instructions are written in the margin or at the end of a document, they are usually placed in a circle to show that they are **not** to be keyed-in/printed.

[3] **Stet** means **'let it stand'** – when the new and original words have **both** been crossed out, key-in the word with the dotted line underneath.

Glossary

Administrative Assistant Provides support to specific departments or teams within an organisation.

Agenda A notice of the time, date and place of a meeting and a list of items to be discussed at the meeting.

Animation A series of still images/text that are linked together as part of a sequence which makes the image/text appear to move.

Back-up A copy of the data held on a network/electronic system made in case the original data is lost or damaged.

Budget A record of money in and money out for an event; also, the amount of money set aside to estimate how much can be spent on an event.

CC An emailing term which means 'carbon copy'. A CC is intended for those people who are not directly involved with the email but may need to see it for information purposes.

Cell reference Each cell in a spreadsheet has a reference that describes its position in the worksheet: row position and column position, e.g. A5 = Column A, Row 5.

Company policy A plan of action adopted by a company designed to make sure that the company operates in a way that meets the requirements of the company, its customers and the law.

Complimentary close The method of closing a business letter, e.g. Yours faithfully if the letter is very formal and you have addressed it to 'Dear Sir or Madam'; Yours sincerely or Yours truly if you have addressed it to 'Dear Mr/Mrs …'

Consistent Making sure all font types, sizes and colours are similar.

Data Words, numbers, etc. which have no particular use or meaning before they are organised into information.

Database Software which stores a variety of related information in an organised manner.

Delegate (noun) A member of a group representing an organisation at an event.

Desktop publishing Software that allows you to lay out pages yourself and move pictures and text around the page.

Edit To change or correct data in a document, spreadsheet, database or other program.

Flat database A single table of information organised in rows (records) and columns (fields) (*see page 56*).

Format (verb) To change the appearance of text and graphics.

Formatting Changing the appearance of text and graphics.

Formula A code which when entered into a cell in a spreadsheet performs a calculation, e.g. =B5+C5.

Graphic A picture or image stored electronically.

Hyperlink A piece of text, graphic or button on a web page which when clicked will take you to another location on the same web page or to another web page, either on the same or another website.

Information Data that has been organised together to have some meaning.

Integrate To include information contained in a document, spreadsheet, database or other program into another document, spreadsheet, database or other program.

Internal network A secure business environment which operates through a Local Area Network (LAN) similar to the World Wide Web, with limited access usually restricted to authorised users such as employees of a particular organisation.

Internet Computers connected worldwide. ('Inter' means 'between' – the internet is a link between various networks.)

Intranet A secure connection with which an organisation can transfer data, letters and files without worrying about confidentiality risks. ('Intra' means 'within' – an intranet is confined within an individual company or organisation.)

Job advert A statement to attract the best potential applicants to a job.

Job analysis A detailed study of the requirements and qualifications necessary to complete a job.

Job description A statement which sets out the purpose of a job; where the job fits into the organisation structure; and the responsibilities and key tasks of the job.

Mail merge A function of software for creating many letters or documents based on a template and a database or table of names and addresses.

Merge field A placeholder (field) can be inserted into a document to show a certain category of information, e.g. address, greeting, date, etc.

Minutes (of a meeting) A summary of all points discussed and all decisions taken during a meeting – they usually include the names of those in attendance and/or absent.

Password A code made up of letters, numbers or a combination of both which must be entered – usually in conjunction with a username – into a computer network to allow access to files stored there.

Person specification A description of the requirements a person needs to be able to perform a particular job satisfactorily, e.g. education and qualifications; training and experience; and personal attributes/qualities.

Personal data Information about someone who is identifiable and living.

Preview In most software packages, this is the function which allows the user to see how a document will look when printed.

Profit The difference between the amount earned and the amount spent in buying, operating or producing something.

Reference A piece of information which helps identify the originators of a piece of business documentation, e.g. a reference on a formal business letter is usually comprised of two pieces of information: the initials of the person who will sign the letter and the initials of the person preparing it, such as JS/AA.

Relational database An electronic database consisting of two or more tables (*see Flat database*) of related information allowing a link between the tables so that the two can be searched simultaneously.

Research To use books or the internet to find information to solve a problem or find out extra information about a specific topic.

Salutation The beginning of a formal business letter, e.g. Dear Sir, or Dear Mr Smith or Dear John.

Select recipients (in mail merge) To connect the document to a data source or a data file by using an existing list (table) with relevant information or by creating a list (table) of information.

Spreadsheet A type of software used to carry out calculations using text, values and formulae.

Standard document A document which includes page formatting, text and graphics.

Template A standard document with pre-set layouts and formats into which the user simply inserts the text required.

Transition In presentation software such as PowerPoint® this is the visual movement as one slide changes to another.

WiFi Use of radio channels to connect to the internet. Publicly available WiFi links to the internet are called 'hot spots' and may be found in airports, train stations and some cafés.

Wizard An automatic creation of pre-set templates which enables users to make the best use of the available facilities and use complex features of software programs which they wouldn't be able to do otherwise.

Index